HELPING COUPLES

*Proven Strategies for
Coaches, Counselors & Clergy*

Drs. Les & Leslie Parrott
Dr. David H. Olson

ZONDERVAN
BOOKS

ZONDERVAN BOOKS

Helping Couples
Copyright © 2021 by The Foundation for Healthy Relationships

Requests for information should be addressed to:
Zondervan, *3900 Sparks Dr. SE, Grand Rapids, Michigan 49546*

Zondervan titles may be purchased in bulk for educational, business, fundraising, or sales promotional use. For information, please email SpecialMarkets@Zondervan.com.

ISBN 978-0-310-36356-9 (softcover)
ISBN 978-0-310-36358-3 (audio)
ISBN 978-0-310-36357-6 (ebook)

Any internet addresses (websites, blogs, etc.) and telephone numbers in this book are offered as a resource. They are not intended in any way to be or imply an endorsement by Zondervan, nor does Zondervan vouch for the content of these sites and numbers for the life of this book.

Published in association with Yates & Yates, www.yates2.com.

Cover image: Melpomenem / iStockphoto
Interior design: Phoebe Wetherbee

Printed in the United States of America

21 22 23 24 25 /LSC/ 10 9 8 7 6 5 4 3 2 1

Dedicated to the thousands of marriage champions on the front lines with couples who are engaged, in distress, or simply moving from good to great. This one is for you.

CONTENTS

INTRODUCTION

AN ENCOURAGING WORD TO MARRIAGE CHAMPIONS

It takes two flints to make a fire.
—*Louisa May Alcott*

We met each other for the first time on a sweltering summer day in New Orleans. We were attending the 1989 Annual Convention of the American Psychological Association. For more than a hundred years, this gathering has been the epicenter for cutting-edge social science research and practice. More than ten thousand attend this super bowl of psychology and choose from hundreds of workshops and sessions.

As an eager graduate student, I (Les) was nearing the finish line of my doctoral dissertation. The topic was love. That's right. I did a scholarly study, involving hundreds of people, on the mushy subject of love. And I was making my first professional presentation to a scant handful of sympathetic attendees who, in all honesty, were likely more invested in supporting a fledgling social scientist than they were in the findings of my research.

In another part of the convention center, David held a packed ballroom spellbound by talking about how to predict marital success through his groundbreaking Circumplex Model. Leslie and I had studied this renowned tool in our clinical training, so of course we wanted to hear about it firsthand from the originator, David, himself.

That's how our relationship began. Two research junkies—a neophyte and a master—who spoke each other's language. Over the years, we have crisscrossed at more conferences, spoken from the same stage, discussed research on the phone, reviewed one another's writings, and basically geeked out on all things marriage.

That's why, after decades of study and research, we feel compelled to summarize what we have learned. It's why we've written this book. We want to show you what we know for sure about the science of lasting love.

Did you catch that?

We're not just writing about love. We're writing about love over a lifetime. We want to reveal the secrets behind couples who go the distance. Our focus is on how to build an abiding bond that endures even the inevitable tough times and comes out stronger. Our focus is on *lasting* love.

Putting the Cookies on the Bottom Shelf

Allow us to put your mind at ease. You don't need to be a scholar or a statistician to read this book. We aren't writing to impress. We're writing to support. This book is for amateurs and experts alike. It's primary goal? To help you help couples. You may be a member of the clergy, a professional counselor, a new trainee, or a volunteer who is coaching or mentoring couples. You are our kind of people, and our life's work has been dedicated to helping you.

Though we don't know you personally, we know at least two things about you. First, you want to make a positive difference in the lives of couples. Second, you are traveling at the speed of life and possibly overscheduled. We get that. It's the nature of your work. That's why this book is not an exhaustive text you'll need to wade through to find a tidbit of information you can put into practice. Nope. This book is brief and to the point—chock-full of proven knowledge, evidence-based methods, and practical strategies. You simply need to take the information in this book off the proverbial shelf and start using it.

We're avoiding psychobabble, pat answers, and academic jargon. Instead, we are dedicated to summing up the most important and practical applications you can use with the couples in your care. Our mantra while writing each chapter has been *clarity and accessibility*. We want to simplify the complicated and make it easy to use.

Knowing What Really Works

One more thing you need to know as we get started—we're not giving you our opinions. We're writing about what empirical research reveals.[1] Why? First, because we are steeped in the professional literature, evidence-based studies published in peer-reviewed journals. And second, because the three of us have had access to some of the largest research pools on the planet. What we are about to show you comes from information, surveys, and studies involving what we've learned from more than five million couples.

If you're wondering how that could be, let us explain.

In 1980, I (David), while teaching at the University of Minnesota, founded a program called PREPARE/ENRICH (P/E). It started as a paper-and-pencil questionnaire that couples would complete with the help of a facilitator and mail in to be tabulated. Eventually, of course, the questionnaire was digitized and moved online. Little did I know that P/E would become one of the most widely used assessments for couples around the world. It's now used in more than 140,000 churches and by more than 60,000 professional counselors with millions of couples.

In 2000, we (Les and Leslie) were among the cofounders of a groundbreaking online enterprise spearheaded by Neil Clark Warren, PhD. Its purpose? To help people find the love of their life. We called it eHarmony. At one point, an average of more than 230 weddings a day were taking place because of matches made through the scientific matching methods of eHarmony. This gave us so much data on couples that we established eHarmony Labs and invited some of the top relationship researchers from schools including Harvard, Stanford, University of Chicago, UCLA, and so on, to join us in learning everything we could.

And in 2010, we received news from our publisher that our book for engaged couples, *Saving Your Marriage Before It Starts*, had been used by more than a million couples. That's an important publishing milestone, and it was the catalyst for a national listening tour of marriage champions. We wanted to discover what would help them do their work more effectively. The result? We ended up launching an online tool called the SYMBIS Assessment, designed especially for marriage champions using our *Saving Your Marriage Before It Starts* curriculum. Again, this gave us access to a very significant pool of research data on couples.*

So, here we are, three marriage-research nerds that feel

---

* All user information is encrypted and abstracted from users' identities using industry best practices.

compelled to share with you what we have learned from all of this—our own research as well as that of countless colleagues. It would be easy, in some respects, to just do our own thing. After all, we are founders of two different assessment tools—and they both serve the same audience. Some might even see our two assessments as competitors, like Ford and Chevy. Not us. The cause is too big for that. We are driven by a mission. An alliance. Collectively, we want to continue to make an even bigger dent in the divorce rate—together. We are motivated by people like you, regardless of what resources you might favor. We agree with entrepreneur J. C. Penney when he said, "The best teamwork comes from those who are working independently toward one goal in unison." That's true of us and our relationship with you, a marriage champion. We are all in this together—helping couples build lasting love.

We Can't Say This Enough

Now, we want to say something that, for us, is the most important message in this book. Two words: *Thank you*. Don't for a minute think we say this flippantly. We're not adding on a "gracious" little note to the end of this introduction because it seems appropriate or proper. This *thank you* comes from the heart. We are overwhelmed by the work you do, and we are so grateful that you do it.

We've heard from you—or someone just like you—nearly every day for years upon years. We receive your questions, clarifications, and sometimes your desperations involving a sticky situation. And sometimes we hear from you because you can't contain your enthusiasm over the success of a new technique or insight. We pull for you. And often pray for you. In fact, we've written every word on every page of this book with you in mind.

In a very real sense, this entire book is a huge *thank you* for the countless sessions, classes, and groups where you have helped couples at every age and stage. Chances are that you've prepared yourself to be the best kind of marriage champion you can be, and you continue to do so. You wouldn't be reading this book if that weren't the case.

If you've been at this for any length of time, you've likely disrupted your own dinner to take a call from a couple in need. Maybe you've rearranged your schedule to accommodate a couple in crisis. If you've worked with engaged couples, you've likely had to bite your tongue and simply nod in an effort to build rapport while a misguided couple reveals unrealistic ideals.

At times, you've carried the burden of another's aching heart so much that it affected your own. You've kept confidences and crafted strategies for the couples in your care. You've also reviewed an intervention or a teaching point on your drive home from the office and a little sting caused you to mutter to yourself, "I can do that better next time." And you do.

You've also had a front row seat to the sometimes seemingly miraculous. You've watched couples who were on the brink of blowing a family to pieces heal hurts and rejoin their spirits. You've protected and helped children you've never even met by helping their parents love each other better.

Or maybe you are a marriage champion in training. Maybe

you are on the brink of becoming a counselor or coach, or maybe you are entering the ministry. Perhaps you're a grad student plugging away on a research project to add value to the guild. Regardless, you are dedicating yourself to help couples—engaged couples launch lifelong love, or couples in distress find solutions that seem beyond their reach. You may even be focused on helping higher-functioning couples move from good to great.

Wherever you are in your experience, your training, or your focus, we want you to know this: *You are doing more good than you will ever know.* And we are beyond grateful for your service. You may never hear it from those you help, though we hope you do. But never for a moment forget how valuable you are to couples wanting to enjoy lifelong love. You are changing lives, and your efforts have a ripple effect that may even change generations. "The greatest use of a life is to spend it on something that will outlast it," said nineteenth-century psychologist William James. And that's exactly what you're doing.

We wish we knew you personally. We wish we knew your name. If we did, you'd see it printed on the dedication page of this book. You are the reason this research matters. The decades we've spent gaining insights and knowledge from studies are so we could give it to you—with heartfelt gratitude.

1

LOVE IS NOT ENOUGH

We all eat lies when our hearts are hungry.
—*Penelope Douglas*

What makes a good marriage? If you're like nearly 90 percent of the population, we know your answer: "Being in love."[1] A good marriage, people say, is built on a powerful romantic attraction, fueled by companionship, and empowered by happiness. Nobody thinks about getting married in hopes that love may eventually show up. We don't think of getting married to find intimacy as a bonus. Not these days, anyway. We get married because we're in love.

For most of history, however, love wasn't the motivator. It had little to do with it. People had modest expectations of marital happiness. Instead of love, people married throughout history to form alliances between families, gain economic support, or expand the family labor force.

But as family plots of land gave way to market economies and kingdoms ceded power to democracies, the notion of marriage changed with the times. Today, marriage is seen as a bond that's all about love and intimacy. Romance is the essential precursor to marriage. We see it as a requirement. We see it as paramount. What's more, most see marriage as a means to more happiness. In fact, it holds a magical key, many believe, to "living happily ever after."[2]

And that's the problem. As you know, marriage, no matter how loving, isn't a fairy tale. Nobody, not a prince or princess, will forever embody everything a person ever wanted. The "perfect" person, their "soul mate," eventually lets them down. "You're not the person I married," they say. Which is precisely why too many couples call it quits on their love story before attempting to write a new chapter in their marriage. They buy the lie that says romantic love is all you need, and they end up choking on disappointment.

We have been poisoned by fairy tales.

—Anaïs Nin

In 2001, we (Les and Leslie) received a call from the governor of Oklahoma. Why? The Sooner State, as it turns out, was experiencing a sky-high divorce rate. So much so that it was eroding the state's economy. And that gets a politician's attention. We accepted the governor's invitation to move from Seattle to Oklahoma for a year to serve as his "marriage ambassadors." We began our one-year stint by, among other things, interviewing couples in nearly every county of the state. And whenever we encountered an engaged couple, we'd ask the same question: "What are you doing for marriage preparation?" The answer became predictable. It was almost always something along these lines: "Oh, we don't need any counseling; we're in love and that's enough."

You've heard the same thing from couples in your care. And if only it were true. But scientific studies don't agree—as if you needed research to make this point for you. You already know marriage is not an elongated honeymoon. "When choosing a long-term partner," says founder of Collaborative Couple Therapy, Dan Wile, "you will inevitably be choosing a particular set of unsolvable problems."[3] Marriage takes sacrifice, hard work, and the ability to put up with disappointment and cope with frustration. Not only that, every good marriage, no matter how good, eventually bumps into bad things. And romantic love, no matter how idyllic, is not enough to sustain it.

As a marriage champion, you are pushing against the current of the culture when you try to help couples understand this. So we dedicate this chapter to helping you ride the rapids of romance with skill. We'll show you what research says about the true requirements for a good marriage and how you can help couples find a better way. But first, we delve into the overarching reason this generation is in desperate need of what you have to offer.

What's Wrong with Romance?

When asked to list the essential ingredients of love as a basis for marriage, a survey of more than a thousand college students revealed that "no single item was mentioned by at least one half of those responding." In other words, people can't agree on what love is. Or perhaps more accurately, people don't really *know* what love is. They just know it when they *feel* it. As one person in the survey said, "Love is like lightning: you may not know what it is, but you do know when it hits you."

We all get that. After all, romance is ingrained into our consciousness from an early age by countless poems, songs, films, and fantasies. Pop culture makes the message clear: The dizzying and all-consuming experience of romance is at

> *Passion, though a bad regulator, is a powerful spring.*
>
> —Ralph Waldo Emerson

the heart of love.[4] No wonder we think it's all we need for marriage.

Of course, as social scientists—no, strike that—as people who have simply been married for a few years, we all know that love, the kind that lasts, is far more than a heart-skips-a-beat sensation. Yet still this notion persists for far too many good-intentioned couples—even experienced couples who are marrying for the second or third time.[5]

In case you're wondering, we have nothing against romance. We resonate with philosophical poet Percy Bysshe Shelley who wrote, "Soul meets soul on lovers' lips." Romance is vital to a happy marriage. Science has been pretty tough on romance. We'll admit it. But it's simply saying that it's not nutrient dense. Romance in marriage is unquestionably delicious, but it's dessert, not the main course. Romance alone can't fortify longevity.

When people say "being in love" is the key to marriage, knowingly or not, they equate it to romance. And the more someone relies on romance to support their relationship, the more deluded and disappointed they become.

When neuroscientists examined the brains of people in romantic love, they found that the areas of the brain involved with decision making and judgment become impaired.[6] A person who claims to be "truly, deeply, and madly" in love actually activates brain regions associated with delusion, drug craving, and addiction.[7] Powerful, right? Then again, we've all had this inkling. Long before these sophisticated studies were conducted, even fifteenth-century poet Pedro Calderón de la Barca had inklings: "When love is not madness, it is not love."[8]

Why Romantic Love Is Not Enough

When romantic love is mistaken for lasting love, we marry an idealized image of our partner. That person doesn't exist in real life. And in time, marriage asks us to look reality squarely in the face and reckon with the fact that we did not marry the person we thought we did.

Each of us constructs an idealized image of the person we marry. The image is painted by our partner's eager efforts to put their best foot forward, but it takes root in the rich soil of our romantic fantasies. We want to see our partner at their best. We imagine, for example, that they would never become irritable or put on excess weight. We focus on what we find admirable and blank out every blemish. The lens of romance causes us to see them as more noble, more attractive, more intelligent, more gifted than they really are. But not for long. Why? Because romance is fueled by feelings. And feelings are always fluid.

> *The art of love is largely the art of persistence.*
>
> —Albert Ellis

Romantic love, by its very nature, is fleeting. Some believe the half-life of romantic love is about three months, after which you have only half the amount of romantic feelings you started out with.[9] Others believe romantic love stays at a peak for two to three years before starting to fade.[10] Whichever theory is correct, be assured that the enchantment of romance eventually and most certainly doesn't last. Mutual idealizing gives way to mutual disillusionment. After all, no human being can fulfill an idealized dream. Letdown is inevitable.

Don't worry, there's good news. Sunshine can be found

behind the dark clouds of disappointment. And every marriage champion can help couples find it. Once a couple realizes that marriage is not the source of constant romance, they begin to appreciate the fleeting moments of romance for what they are— very special experiences. It's what journalist Mignon McLaughlin was getting at when she said, "A successful marriage requires falling in love many times, always with the same person."

Strangely, the moment a couple realizes this is the moment they find what they were hoping for all along. Their disenchantment, once accepted as a sign of growth, not despair, enables them to move into deeper and enduring intimacy. And if there's one thing we know from our studies, it's this: You can help them do just that. You can facilitate this mystical morphing of emotions. You can enable a starry-eyed couple to see more clearly and capture this new vision.

In your pre-marriage work, you've seen dozens, if not hundreds, of couples in your office or classroom. And if you've been doing this for more than a decade, maybe you've become a bit jaded by their naivete. That's understandable. But don't think your work is futile. These couples need you.

Forty percent of respondents in a recent survey stated that romance was essential to them because they could not feel love without it.[11] What they don't know, of course, is that love is more than a feeling. That's where you come in.

Helping Couples See More Clearly

According to acclaimed marriage researcher John Gottman, "Couples wait an average of six years of being unhappy before getting help."[12] Think about that. Couples let problems and resentments fester for years before seeking help from someone like you. For this reason alone, your efforts to help couples on the front end—to save marriages before they start—is crucial.

And did you know that almost two-thirds of divorces happen within the first ten years of marriage?[13] Think of the heartache you can help engaged couples avoid by helping them start smart. The question, of course, is how? In a sense, this entire book is dedicated to answering that question, but for now we want to put the emphasis on one word: *expectations.*

At the touch of love everyone becomes a poet.

—Plato

"Blessed is he who expects nothing," said eighteenth-century poet Alexander Pope, "for he shall never be disappointed." Okay. Well, maybe. Then again, maybe not. Do we really want couples on the brink of marriage to expect nothing? Of course not. Besides that, it's impossible. New couples are ripe with expectations about money, sex, in-laws, holidays, chores, communication, conflict, decor, friendships, vacations, spirituality, roles, careers, you name it. There's no shortage of expectations. And when they are unreasonable or misaligned, heartache is soon to follow. Why? Because unfulfilled expectations dismantle the fantasy of the proverbial fairy tale that's been fueled by feelings. "'And they lived happily ever after' is one of the most tragic sentences in literature," said rabbi and author Joshua Liebman. "It's tragic because it's a falsehood. It is a myth that has led generations to expect something from marriage that is not possible."

One thing we know for sure: *The majority of new couples distort their view of their relationship in a positive direction because of faulty expectations.*

How do we know? Because we've measured the phenomenon using the Evaluation and Nurturing Relationship Issues, Communication, and Happiness Scale.[14] It's a mouthful, for sure. That's why we call it ENRICH. And over the decades, it's been used by thousands of fellow researchers in a variety of studies to better understand what we call the "rose-colored glasses syndrome."[15]

As one example, researchers at Fort Hays State University, using ENRICH and our Marital Satisfaction Scale, along with its two subscales of Idealistic Distortion and Marital Satisfaction, found expectations to be of prime importance because of the large discrepancy between what many couples see as the ideal marriage and what actually takes place.[16] Studies like this have been replicated hundreds of times.[17] The rose-colored phenomenon is indisputable.

Recalibrating Great Expectations

Don't mistake your job as a marriage champion as finding a remedy by replacing distorted expectations with lowered expectations. We are not saying couples need to lower their expectations. In fact, we cringe at the thought. Reasonable couples don't need to expect less in their relationship. In all likelihood they need to aspire higher. Why? Because reasonable people get what they expect. If you have low expectations for marriage, your relationship will surely suffer. If you expect your spouse to treat you poorly, he or she will. Conversely, having reasonably high standards for your marriage increases the chances that your marriage will excel.[18]

Expectations are only problematic when they are misaligned ("I thought *you* were going to pay the bills") or unreasonable ("You should *always* make me happy").[19] Therefore, the goal is to simply get expectations into the open and get them rectified or aligned. Eli Finkel, professor at Northwestern University, and many others call it "recalibrating" marital expectations.

> *Life is so constructed, that the event does not, cannot, will not, match the expectation.*
>
> —Charlotte Brontë

Research makes it abundantly clear: expectations are deeply linked to marital satisfaction. It's one of the reasons our *Saving Your Marriage Before It Starts* (SYMBIS) curriculum begins with helping couples uncover the "Myths of Marriage."[20] What are these myths? Here are the top four.

Myth One: "We Expect Exactly the Same Things from Marriage"

Every relationship is governed by a list of unspoken rules. Things like "always be on time," "don't talk about your feelings," or "downplay your success." Everybody has them. We either inherit our unspoken rules or invent them. And only when our spouse "breaks" them do we even know they exist. On top of that, they are often powered by unconscious role expectations. Like an actor following a dramatic script, we act out roles formed unconsciously through a blend of personality traits and family systems. These roles create deeply felt expectations for what a husband or wife should do, think, or feel. And helping couples align mismatched expectations shaped by unspoken rules and unconscious roles can make a marriage.

Myth Two: "Everything Good in Our Relationship Will Get Better"

While many things improve in relationships, some become more difficult. Every successful marriage requires necessary losses. For some it's a rite of passage that means giving up the freedoms of youth. For others it means giving up a carefree lifestyle and coming to terms with new limits and inconveniences. In other words, marriage is filled with both enjoyable and tedious trade-offs. But by far, the most dramatic loss experienced in a new marriage, as we have shown, is the idealized image of a partner.

Myth Three: "Everything Bad in My Life Will Disappear"

This myth has been handed down through generations and is epitomized in storybook legends. Many believe marriage will erase pain, bring healing, or eliminate loneliness. But as we know, when a couple leaves a wedding, they remain the same people. A marriage certificate is not a magical glass slipper. Complaints about matrimony arise not because life is worse than before, but because it is not incomparably better.

Myth Four: "My Spouse Will Make Me Whole"

Marriage challenges every spouse to be a better person, but neither marriage nor a partner will magically make someone complete. Marriage is not a shortcut to personal wellbeing or emotional health. This false expectation, in fact, leads some to become dependent on their partner in a way that is by all standards unhealthy. They create *enmeshed* relationships, characterized by overdependence and a strong dose of low self-esteem. This deeply flawed expectation may be the most dangerous myth of all.

Helping couples align their expectations by avoiding these kinds of myths is key to getting them started on the right foot. We'll say it again: A mountain of research reveals that marital satisfaction is inexorably linked to marital expectations. And if you're not helping couples recalibrate expectations, they will be prone to thinking romantic love is enough.

> When two people are under the influence of the most violent, most insane, most delusive, and most transient of passions, they are required to solemnly swear they will remain in that excited, abnormal, and exhausting condition continuously until death do them part.
>
> —George Bernard Shaw

"One should always be in love," quipped Oscar Wilde, "that is the reason one should never marry." We beg to differ. And in the next chapter, we'll show you why.

2

THE 31 PERCENT FACTOR

It is a capital mistake to theorize
before one has data.
—*Sir Arthur Conan Doyle*

The first documented premarital intervention was in 1922. Ernest Groves, a graduate of Yale and Dartmouth, began counseling engaged students at Boston University. Professor Groves, a sociologist, served for a short time as a pastor in Maine, but teaching and researching soon became his life's work. He wrote the first college text on the subject, simply called *Marriage*, in 1933. He even held a successful annual marriage conference for couples, along with his wife, Gladys, who was a notable author as well. Gladys and Ernest were a writing-teaching-counseling team.[1] But it was not until Professor Groves developed the first college credit course in marriage preparation at Boston University did any professionals turn their attention to helping engaged couples.

Of course, marriage has always been with us, dating back to Old Testament times, more than four thousand years ago. The first evidence of wedding ceremonies dates from about 2350 BC, in Mesopotamia.[2] But not until the twentieth century did we get serious about helping these new couples.

The first mention of premarital education as a significant process or valuable service was in a 1928 article in the *American Journal of Obstetrics and Gynecology*.[3] The article concluded: "The clear-cut duty of the doctor, before wedding days are fixed, is to forestall trouble, and to seek occasions for forestalling trouble."[4] Okay. Not terribly insightful. But it was a start.

In 1941, the Philadelphia Marriage Council established the

first standardized program with the stated purpose to help young married and premarital couples gain "a better understanding of what companionship in married life involves and thus help them avoid some of the causes of marital difficulties."[5]

Those difficulties, unfortunately, seemed, more often than not, focused on how wives should "look after" their husbands: "Plan dinner the night before. Never complain. Speak with a soft voice."[6] This cringeworthy advice from the 1950s surely caused more problems than it helped.

Despite these fledgling beginnings, premarital education began to get more relevant in the 1970s. That's when clergy started meeting with couples prior to their wedding. It was a good step, but it took another decade or two before these meetings shifted from talking mostly about the wedding ceremony and the meaning of marriage to the more practical aspects of real life as a married couple.[7] Also, up until this same time, professional counselors tended to treat individuals only. They might process marriage struggles regarding a spouse, but they typically did not see couples together.

> *Those who ignore statistics are condemned to reinvent them.*
>
> —Brad Efron

Things have changed. And it's no coincidence that a heightened interest in marriage education emerged around the same time that the divorce rate was increasing. In fact, as the need became more and more apparent, a "marriage movement" was born.[8] Religious leaders, professional counselors, scholars, educators, researchers, authors, and even politicians recognized the need to help couples before and after they marry.[9]

As a professional community, we know more today about what it takes to make marriage work than we've ever known.[10] And this chapter is dedicated to showing you exactly what that means. In fact, as we answer the most common questions we hear on the subject, you'll soon see how *the work you are doing is decreasing a couple's chances of divorce by at least 31 percent.*

But first, a couple of preliminary and important questions.

Is Marriage Still a Value?

Almost every day you hear about a celebrity couple calling it quits on their marriage, not to mention a couple in your own neighborhood or social circle. And, of course, there's the rising rates of cohabitation and talk of how it's replacing marriage. Some commentators and bloggers startle with headlines about marriage being "quaint" or "obsolete." Sociologists of a certain stripe tout the so-called benefits of divorce and talk about "starter marriages" that are expected to end within the first five years.[11] It's enough to make you wonder if the idea of a committed marriage is actually dying.

It's not. Sure, there may be more singles today and people marrying at a later age, but nearly everyone, regardless of their socioeconomic status or cultural background, puts a high value on marriage. In fact, they value marriage not only as a social institution but as a personal goal. As Harvard professor Martin Whyte points out, America is still "very marriage prone."[12] There's little evidence of rejection of marriage as an institution, according to Whyte. Polls report that 95 percent of Americans say they want to marry and think they will. Not only that, they want it to be married for life. But if a pollster asks, "Can a woman or a man have a full and complete life without ever getting married?" the answer is also *yes*. Nearly 75 percent of those surveyed agreed with this view. People still want to get married, but the urgency or the sense that it's necessary or that you can't have a full life without getting married has changed.[13]

High divorce rates, nonmarital childbearing rates, and cohabitation may testify to the vulnerability of marriage. But rest assured that the vast majority of people still value a committed and loving marriage relationship. And with good reason. Marriage is good for you. The happiest and healthiest people on the planet are married.[14] Quietly, with little fanfare, a broad and deep body of scientific literature has been accumulating that affirms: it is not good for man—or woman—to be alone. In virtually every way that social scientists can measure, married people do much better than the unmarried or divorced: they live longer, healthier, happier, sexier, and more affluent lives.[15]

> *In every marriage more than a week old, there are grounds for divorce. The trick is to find and continue to find grounds for marriage.*
>
> —Robert Anderson

Want more good news? The couples who are contemplating marriage want what you have to offer. Of the 2.5 million couples who wed each year in America, more than a third of them want some form of marriage education.[16] In fact, 44 percent of couples today report having received some form of premarital education, typically provided by a religious organization.[17] People used to marry because they had to. Today it's a choice. People are more intentional about it and more motivated to do it right.

"It's hard to overestimate the function of choice in this," says Dudley Rose, assistant dean for ministry studies at Harvard Divinity School. "When marriage involves social or economic necessity, one cannot fully *choose* the institution or its obligations. But when you commit without pressure, then mutual consent takes on new meaning."[18] Marriage may change. It may evolve. But marriage is a treasured value and will not go away.

What Do Singles Think about Marriage?

This question may not be top of mind, but it's important because attitudes toward marriage have shifted significantly over recent decades.[19] The better you understand these attitudes, the more effective you'll be as a champion. We (Les and Leslie), working with a research team at the University of Chicago, interviewed more than 3,600 young adults, ages eighteen to thirty, to understand a wide swath of information: their intent to marry and/or have children, childhood family background, life goals, values, current expectations of marriage, reasons for and against marriage, attitudes toward divorce, opinions about what holds a marriage together and what breaks it apart, cohabitation, and so on.

What did we find? We discovered several distinct attitudinal sets, or what we have come to call the five Marriage Mindsets:

- *Resolute—purposeful, determined, and unwavering.* This segment, 22 percent of the population, prizes marriage and holds tight to an unyielding determination for making it go the distance. When it comes to marriage, they are dedicated to ensuring that it's for life.
- *Rational—logical, sound judgment, and realistic.* This segment, 23 percent of the population, takes a more practical approach to marriage than most. They view this lifelong commitment with more caution than others.
- *Romantic—inspired by the ideal of affection and love.* This segment, 19 percent of the population, brings a heavy dose of *idealism* to marriage. Romantics expect love to be lived out with unending passion and ongoing intimacy. Love, for the Romantic, is a bit like a movie. It is adventurous, poetic, starry-eyed, chivalrous.
- *Restless—cavalier, in no hurry, and unsettled.* This segment, 22 percent of the population, isn't so sure about marriage—at least for now. This group is dominated by males who aren't ready to settle down because they are busy exploring their options. From their perspective, the fewer responsibilities they take on, including marriage, the more fun they believe they'll have.
- *Reluctant—resistant and unwilling.* This segment, 14 percent of the population, is "not the marrying kind." More than any other segment, Reluctants are cynical about matrimony. In fact, it's the only segment to lack a desire to wed, probably because their own homes were examples of how not to do it.

Most of the individuals you see in pre-marriage counseling will be in the first three mindsets: Resolute, Rational, or Romantic. Each of these three is motivated to be married. The Restless and the Reluctant, not so much. But they'll still show up on occasion. For example, a Restless will appear when external pressures have moved them to marry—an unplanned pregnancy, for example. And you'll even see a Reluctant in your office because their partner wants them there.[20]

Does Marriage Education Really Help Couples?

"The purpose of life," said Robert Kennedy, "is to contribute in some way to making things better." Do you sometimes wonder if your efforts, your contributions, are doing just that? From the marriage champions we've spoken with over the years—clergy, professional counselors, personal coaches, marriage mentors, and educators—we know this is a common question. We know you sometimes wonder if what you are doing for couples is really making a difference.

> *Marriage is a book of which the first chapter is written in poetry and the remaining chapters in prose.*
>
> —Beverley Nichols

Wonder no more. Hundreds of studies show that marriage education and counseling make a significant positive difference for the majority of couples.[21]

The evidence is overwhelming. Programs providing marriage-skills training help couples increase happiness, improve their relationships, and avoid negative behaviors that can lead to marital breakup.[22]

If you've ever taken a course in statistics, you've heard of "meta-analysis." If not, it's easy to understand. Meta-analysis is a procedure for combining data from multiple studies. In other words, it draws overarching and accurate conclusions of previous research studies to help us see a bigger picture. It draws empirical conclusions from numerous studies, not just one. In other words, and specific to our topic, it helps us identify a common effect of marriage education.

And one of the most highly respected studies of this kind was conducted by Scott Stanley at the University of Denver, along with his associates. Their landmark study, across four states, provides ample evidence that marriage education, training, and counseling programs—some of which have been around for more than forty years—significantly strengthened the marriages of couples who have taken advantage of such programs. These studies, integrating findings from well over one hundred separate evaluations, show that a wide variety of marriage-strengthening programs can reduce strife, improve communication, increase parenting skills, and increase stability. "More precisely," the study found, "the odds ratio indicated that premarital education was associated with a decline of 31 percent in the annual odds of divorce."[23] You may want to read that sentence again. This is significant. The premarital couples you serve are reducing their chances of divorce by 31 percent. That's a major wedding gift.

Another analysis that integrated eighty-five studies

involving nearly four thousand couples enrolled in more than twenty different marriage-enrichment programs found that the average couple, after participating in a program, was better off than more than two-thirds of couples who did not participate.[24] Yet another analysis, examining over twenty-three separate studies, revealed that the average program participant was significantly better off than 79 percent of nonparticipants. They documented that participants experienced gains in the areas of interpersonal skills and overall relationship quality.[25]

A study that I (David) conducted with Luke Knutson documents the effectiveness of premarital inventory questionnaires and counseling in preventing marital distress. This approach yielded a 52 percent increase in the number of couples classified as "most satisfied" with their relationship. Among the remaining couples, more than half improved their assessment of their relationship. Among the highest-risk couples, more than 80 percent moved up into a more positive category.[26] A personalized assessment, as we'll see in the next chapter, is key to this success.

A final study involving premarital couples is worth noting. Jason Carroll at Brigham Young University and William Doherty at the University of Minnesota conducted a comprehensive and critical evaluation of outcome studies exploring the effectiveness of premarital practices. What did they find? *The average person who participated in a premarital education program was significantly better off afterward than 79 percent of people who did not participate.* Not bad, right? Stated another way, people who experience premarital interventions see about a 30 percent increase in measures of outcome success, meaning the quality of their relationship improves significantly.[27]

Key to this kind of positive impact is having the couple fully engaged in the experience (we'll say more about this in the next chapter).[28]

The bottom line is this: Your efforts to help couples are lowering their chances of divorce and increasing their levels of satisfaction. You can't ask for more than that. So the next time you wonder if you're making a difference in the lives of couples, the answer is a resounding *yes*!

Does Cohabitation Help or Hurt?

Since 1960, America has witnessed a twelvefold increase in cohabitation from 430,000 couples to 5.4 million couples. Most couples today, at least two-thirds, live together before getting married.[29] They see it as the best way to "test out" the relationship and increase their odds of doing well in marriage.[30] In fact, the National Marriage Project at the University of Virginia found that nearly half of twentysomethings agreed with the statement, "You would only marry someone if he or she agreed to live together with you first, so that you could find out whether you really get along." About two-thirds said they believed that moving in together before marriage was a good way to avoid divorce.[31]

> *Act as if what you do makes a difference; it does.*
>
> —William James

Sounds logical. But does cohabiting lead to good marriages or the opposite, increasing the likelihood of divorce? Here's what we know: couples who cohabit before marriage (and especially before an engagement) tend to be less satisfied with their marriages and more likely to divorce than couples who do not.[32]

Cohabitation creates what researchers now call "relationship inertia"—when a couple living together ends up in a bad marriage because, well, it's tough to move out once you move in. Merging homes and investing in a joint living space can result in a lot of "sunk costs" that keep couples emotionally and financially tied to relationships that might have ended had the couple not cohabited.

Scott Stanley and Galena Rhoades at University of Denver found that those who moved in together before marriage reported lower marriage satisfaction and more potential for divorce than couples who waited until they were married to make the big move. The researchers posit that the increase in cohabiting couples is resulting in marriages that simply never would have happened in a noncohabiting society.[33]

But the detrimental side of the cohabitation effect is about more than just "inertia." Psychologist Meg Jay, author of *The Defining Decade*, says it's due to "gender asymmetry." Women tend to see cohabiting as a step toward marriage, while some men see it as a way to stall marriage. It is easy to see how such conflicted, often unconscious, motives could be unhealthy.

One thing men and women do agree on, however, is that their standards for a live-in partner are lower than they are for a spouse. Cohabiters want to feel committed to their partners, yet they are often confused about whether they have consciously chosen their mates. Founding relationships on convenience or ambiguity can interfere with the process of claiming the people we love. A life built on top of "maybe you'll do" simply does not feel as dedicated as a life built on top of the "we do" of marriage. As some say, you can't practice permanence.

Scott Stanley calls this effect "sliding, not deciding." Moving from dating to sleeping over to sleeping over a lot to cohabitation is a slow slope, one not marked by rings or ceremonies or sometimes even a conversation. Couples bypass talking about why they want to live together and what it will mean. Most scholars now agree with empirical evidence that shows premarital cohabitation is associated with lower odds of divorce in the first year of marriage but increased odds of divorce in all other years tested, and this finding held across decades.[34]

Another cohabitation study used the PREPARE/ENRICH assessment with 35,684 couples and discovered that cohabitation correlates with less satisfaction in the relationship. While 51 percent of the dating couples living apart were "Vitalized" (most happy type), only 21 percent of the dating couples cohabiting were "Vitalized." Conversely, almost half (48 percent) of the cohabiting dating couples were "Conflicted" (most problematic type), while only 16 percent of noncohabiting dating couples were "Conflicted."[35]

You will find studies pointing to the benefits of living together before marriage. But in truth, those benefits evaporate after the first year of marriage. Over the long run, cohabitation is associated with greater hazards of marital instability and negative relationship outcomes. Premarital cohabitation is viewed as a risk factor for divorce as it predicts later marital instability, poorer marriage quality, and less relationship satisfaction.[36] Compared to married couples, cohabiting couples who eventually marry argue more, have more trouble resolving conflicts, are more insecure about their partners' feelings, and have more problems related to their future goals.[37] As a champion, you can help your couples be deliberate when it comes to deciding, not sliding.

Think of how marriage has morphed since Ernest and Gladys Groves first documented their premarital interventions in New England and conducted their marriage research beginning in the 1920s. Much has changed. In fact, historians believe marriage has changed more in the past fifty years than in the last five thousand.[38] But at the heart of marriage today remains an unquestionable value of committed, lasting love. And your efforts as a marriage champion, much like the efforts of Ernest and Gladys, are impacting countless couples with a ripple effect that is undoubtedly touching future generations. In fact, did you know that for every percentage point the divorce rate drops, the lives of more than a million children are positively impacted? It's true.[39]

So be encouraged.

But aren't you just a little curious? Aren't you wondering if you can do something to make your efforts even more effective—or to at least ensure that your efforts are making a positive difference for every couple you see? We thought so. And we're eager to show you what science has to say about it in the next chapter.

3

AWARENESS IS CURATIVE

The greatest value of a picture is
when it forces us to notice what
we never expected to see.
—*John Tukey*

The year was 1965. You could buy a new car for less than $2,500 and gas it up at just thirty-one cents per gallon. The war in Vietnam was worsening, and Dr. Martin Luther King Jr. was leading a powerful civil rights movement. The latest craze in kids' toys was the skateboard. Women's skirts were getting shorter, and men's hair was getting longer. *The Sound of Music* released in theaters, and you couldn't go anywhere without hearing the Beatles' album, *Help!*

The title was fitting for a new professor at Penn State. I (David) was in my doctoral program and teaching my first marriage course. A researcher at heart, I had to know if the course was effective. Finding nothing of substance in the literature, I put together a research tool I called the Premarital Attitude Scale and gave it to the students before the first lecture and again on the last day of the semester. Turns out it made a positive difference. These promising results got me started on assessments. It was so rewarding to see tangible results of my teaching.

And I wasn't the only one. Word got out and I was eventually asked to do a larger study involving ten agencies that included community groups such as the Catholic Youth Center, Lutheran Social Services, and several local hospitals. This time, I had a variety of different speakers, including PhD students, who presented content to the group of more than one hundred over the course of a half dozen weeks. We taught on all the usual suspects: communication, conflict, intimacy, in-laws, and so on. We were sure this top-quality information was exactly what these couples needed. And we couldn't wait for our pre- and postsurvey to prove it. We could easily envision the proverbial needle of change moving in a positive direction for these couples.

We have a choice: to plow new ground or let the weeds grow.

—Jonathan Westover

But we were wrong. The results of our survey? Not good. No significant gain in information was found. No change in attitude whatsoever. In fact, couples actually got worse. Their conflict resolution abilities seemed to diminish after experiencing the program. Yikes! People liked the lectures just fine, saying they contained good information. High quality. But almost to the person, they said the content wasn't relevant or pertinent to their own relationship. "This just doesn't apply to me," I kept hearing.

You can probably imagine my discouragement. I had to present my findings to the sponsoring agencies. With more than a hundred people in the room, I had to tell them that the effort was a failure. The meeting was terrible. Imagine spending money on an intervention that actually made matters worse! I was peppered with pointed questions that I couldn't always answer, and it crescendoed with the room almost asking in unison, What can we do now?

My answer was honest. I didn't try to dance around the data. "I don't know," I stammered. "I have no idea. But if you'll give me a few months, I'll come up with something." My thinking was that if I could buy some time, I could review the process and uncover something that might help.

And I did. Along with some fellow graduate students, I recalled a common phenomenon that was taking place. When I asked participants to complete the questionnaire of about a hundred items, they were sitting as couples and they wanted to do it together with their partner, not independently. That's when the light bulb turned on for me. I began thinking about the difference it might make if I converted the questions to be about their relationship, instead of an abstract concept. So instead of asking them to rate the importance of the principle of communication, I'd ask how important communication is to their own relationship. That simple change ignited incredible couple conversations. And those conversations were more magical and transforming than the presentations.

Looking back, I realize this is a seemingly subtle and incredibly obvious change, but it made all the difference. That small change transformed their engagement with the content and personalized it to a level I never imagined. This little pivot set me on a pathway that would carry my professional career and enable me to create not only a highly customized tool that I could use in my own research, but a tool that could be used eventually by millions to help couples around the globe personalize and internalize the constructs that are vital to lasting love.

The Difference the Right Assessment Can Make

That first feeble attempt to survey couples with a pre- and postmeasure became the rudiments of what is now called the

PREmarital Personal and Relationship Evaluation, PREPARE for short. In 1968 I accepted a professorship at the University of Maryland where I also became a postdoctoral fellow at the National Institute of Mental Health (NIMH) in Bethesda. Here my research with PREPARE kicked into high gear. Along with numerous associates and doctoral students, I began a series of empirical studies to form a valid and reliable tool that would yield the best results. In fact, we conducted a three-year longitudinal study on couples and marital satisfaction that solidified the value of the instrument.

> *Good counselors lack no clients.*
>
> —Shakespeare

My research eventually brought me to the University of Minnesota in 1973, where I still serve as professor emeritus. Not long into my new assignment, the county received a grant from a local lumber company that wanted to invest in the wellbeing of its community.[1] The idea was to see how marriages could be strengthened, and they wanted to include everyone in the county that applied for a marriage license. This was music to my ears, as you might guess.

The county asked me to head up the study—and I, along with my team, wasted no time. We set up three research groups: a control group that would receive no intervention, a group that would simply receive their assessment report, and a third group that would receive the results of their assessment along with a debriefing of their report from a facilitator, that is, a member of the clergy or a counselor. These facilitators received one day of training from us before walking couples through the pages of their report.

Because the study included so many participants, we computerized the assessment by using IBM cards that could be scanned at the university testing office. I learned to program the scoring in Fortran to create the reports.

The results? They were better than we could have hoped. Reliability and validity measures were rock solid. We were making a dent in the divorce rate, and couples were making measurable improvements in their relationships.

In the autumn of 1977, we officially started PREPARE, meaning we began training workshops for facilitators.[2] We built a system for scale. Air Force chaplains were among the first to integrate it into their services, along with Catholic dioceses, social service groups, and numerous churches of every denomination. The more it was used, the more requests we received for training—even in other countries. It was growing exponentially without a penny of advertising. Clergy and counselors were telling their colleagues, and we hustled to keep up with the requests. My wife, Karen, and I took a second mortgage on our house to rent office space where we could oversee the scorings. Karen ran the office while I continued to run the research and training programs. Scholars from universities far and wide began conducting their own research on the tool too. Soon we had data on couples of varying ethnicities and every socioeconomic level. We started refining the assessment for various groups of couples as well.

In 1980, we expanded the assessment to include married couples, and we called it the *Evaluation and Nurturing Relationship Issues Communication and Happiness*, ENRICH, for short. The PREPARE/ENRICH assessment was now available for couples of any age or stage. What's more, we created special versions for couples expecting a baby, blending a family, cohabiting, serving in the military, in middle age, and so on. We wanted each couple's report to be tailormade and as personalized and relevant as possible. This turned out to be one of its greatest strengths and most desirable features.

For more than four decades, my associates and I have improved and refined the assessment for practitioners like you. It became my life work. Today the tool is used by more than 200,000 facilitators to help millions of couples, and it has been translated into more than a dozen languages.

Why the SYMBIS Assessment?

Let's be clear: When it comes to assessments, we (Les & Leslie) stand on David's shoulders. Make no mistake, he is a pioneer who built the most trusted and effective marriage assessment ever. In fact, we were trained in P/E when we were both in graduate school in the late 1980s. We used it with countless couples throughout our clinical training and eventually at Seattle Pacific University where we taught for twenty-five years. In a sense, we've been with P/E almost from the beginning. David clearly led the way and inspired us to eventually build what we call the SYMBIS Assessment.

But why another assessment? The catalyst came from a massive listening tour we did with a random sample of nearly five hundred marriage champions across North America—each of them a significant user of our *Saving Your Marriage Before It Starts* (SYMBIS) program. At that point, the book and accompanying his/her workbooks (as well as the video teaching) had been used by more than a million couples.[3] We were about to update and revise the research behind it, but before we did, we wondered what marriage champions who were using *Saving Your Marriage Before It Starts*, year in and year out, would like to see changed or improved. What would make their work more effective? So we asked them.

The response was emphatic. They wanted an online assessment tool that would work hand in glove with the curriculum. They wanted to personalize the chapters and exercises in the book and workbooks. So with our working knowledge and relationship research from our years at eHarmony, studying the value of chemistry between two people in a couple, and inspired by David's proven method of training facilitators to debrief a personalized report—along with a great deal of study and investment of resources—we built a customized assessment experience for users of *Saving Your Marriage Before It Starts*.

Standing on David's mountain of research, along with many others, we launched the SYMBIS Assessment for engaged couples in 2014, and two years later the SYMBIS+ Assessment for married couples. We soon learned that marriage champions wanted to use the SYMBIS Assessment whether they used the accompanying *Saving Your Marriage Before It Starts* curriculum or not. That's fine with us. With a special emphasis on the unique personality chemistry within the relationship, our SYMBIS facilitators tell us the tool is engaging, intuitive, and powerful.

> *I do not ask how the wounded one feels; I, myself, become the wounded one.*
>
> —Walt Whitman

We couldn't agree more with George Bernard Shaw when he said: "Imitation is not just the sincerest form of flattery—it's the sincerest form of learning." We have learned and continue to learn more from David than he will ever know.

That's the quick story. And now, for you, it simply comes down to preference, like Ford or Chevy. Both assessments do the job. Both are built on science. They are each data driven. So, simply put, it comes down to which one you prefer.

Why a Proven Assessment Matters

If you are not already trained and certified in either P/E or SYMBIS, you might be wondering why using a proven assessment is so important. Well, the research pretty much speaks for itself.[4]

You've already gathered that *it personalizes the experience of any intervention or educational experience*—regardless of what curriculum or teaching or counseling methods you use. It's true if you are seeing a couple one-on-one or educating couples in a group or large class. It customizes the process like nothing else. An exercise in couple's communication, for example, is no longer a generic or abstract exercise. It's instantly tailored to the chemistry and personalities of two specific people. It reveals personal insights about their communication style. And this kind of personalization goes a long way in ensuring success for your efforts with couples.[5]

Why? Because *customization fuels engagement*. And as you may recall, research reveals that personal engagement can make or break the effectiveness of any marriage education program or counseling intervention. People want to know their results. They are tuned in. I (David) am still amazed when I happen to meet a couple years after they have taken the assessment and they say, "I still remember some of the questions we answered all those years ago."

An assessment also helps you, as a marriage champion, *pinpoint the work you need to zero in on to help a couple or even a group of couples make true progress.* Every couple is unique, of course. And a reliable assessment can reveal what proverbial dials you need to turn for optimal growth and improvement. The assessment makes it concrete and objective. For example, a couple may present a problem of "feeling like we've grown apart," when their report will show you that the true issue is a lack of physical intimacy or maybe divergent views on raising their child. The assessment, like an X-ray, zeroes in on what needs attention.

One of the best ways to prevent divorce is to help high-risk couples either improve their relationship or decide not to get married. And, in fact, 15 percent of couples who go through P/E or SYMBIS with a trained facilitator end up canceling their wedding plans.[6] That's a good thing. Also, a personalized assessment report *provides you with concrete feedback for some of the toughest points of counseling.* If, for example, you know a certain engaged couple really would be served best by pumping the brakes on their wedding plans, an assessment report becomes a mirror you can hold up to them so that they can discover it themselves. You can point to the specifics revealed from answers they provided.

P/E and SYMBIS help you accomplish these kinds of practical gains and many more. But from a macro perspective, both tools help you achieve two vitally important goals: awareness and empathy.

Improved Self-Awareness

Some say that our hearts hold dominion over our heads. In other words, without self-awareness, our emotions rule. We lack objectivity, and the emotional spillover of our conversations clouds our reason. "I was so angry I couldn't think straight," we say.

But not the person who is tuned in to their own emotional experience. Almost as if they are looking into a mirror, they see what others never recognize. They have a grasp on their personal disposition. They know themselves well, their triggers and tendencies. They can explain the reasons behind their most unreasonable emotions.[7] They can step back from their own experience, insert a bit of objectivity, and manifest a level of awareness that helps them pause. Pull back. Regroup. It's a sign of emotional maturity that many never obtain. And those who study it empirically argue that self-awareness is the most fundamental issue in the science of personal growth and wellbeing.[8]

> More than any other single deficiency, I think it is the lack of mutual empathy which results in sword-drawing in marriage.
>
> —Bernard Guerney

Some psychologists call it *metamood*. Sociologists call it *self-observation*. Others call it *mindfulness*. We prefer the term *self-awareness*. Whatever you call it, we're all talking about the attention we give to uncovering our blind spots and acknowledging our internal state. It requires objectivity. And, thankfully, with the right tools and personal insights, objectivity can be learned. It's a skill. And it's precisely what happens when you unpack the personalized pages of a couple's report generated by P/E or SYMBIS. Heightened self-awareness can't help but take place as they learn more about the DNA of their personalities, for example. They can't help but become more objective with their thoughts, actions, ideas, feelings, and interactions. As one of our facilitators put it, "Premarital evaluation gives sight to couples blinded by love."

Deeper Empathy

The capacity to put yourself in the shoes of another person, to see the world from their perspective, is precious and rare. Even in marriage. Can you imagine if we could bottle empathy and give it to every couple as a wedding gift? It would instantly revolutionize the landscape of matrimony. Why? Because empathy is the single greatest relationship skill set a couple can master. It changes everything.

When a spouse accurately understands their partner's situation, feelings, and motives, conflicts are curbed. Intimacy increases. Misunderstandings are few and far between. Two people who read each other well, who are enjoying mutual empathy, have more laughter and less bickering. They offer more care and comfort. They have fewer hurt feelings and more fun. They are less judgmental and more perceptive. They indulge each other's quirks. They find more patience for one another. More forgiveness. An abundance of grace and gratitude. In short, more love.[9]

It's difficult to exaggerate the value of empathy in marriage.

A few years ago, we (Les and Leslie) were part of a gathering of top researchers, about a dozen of us, who shared thoughts and findings on what some are calling the new science of "neural calculus." Now, before we lose you at the very utterance of this mind-numbing phrase, hang in there for just a moment.

Empathy is not new, of course. It's as old as time, but not the way we're talking about it today. Why? Because something new and exciting is brewing in some of the most respected university research laboratories in North America. It's not a cure for a biological disease, but it just may be a cure for whatever's ailing the marriages you're trying to help. We don't say that glibly. It's a fact.

You see, until now neuroscience has studied just one brain at a time. But now two are being analyzed at once, unveiling a never-before-seen neural duet between the brains of a husband and wife as they interact.[10] So why does this matter? Because this emerging new science holds startling implications for every marriage champion. It holds revolutionary secrets for helping a couple bond brain to brain and heart to heart—quite literally.

In fact, Carl Marci of Harvard University has extracted from his extensive data something he calls a "logarithm for empathy."[11] It's all about the interplay of two people as they enjoy a deep connection of rapport. Not only that, his logarithm reduces the pattern of two people's physiology at the peak of rapport—where each feels deeply understood by the other—to a mathematical equation.

Don't worry, we're not about to extrapolate a numerical equation for empathy here. We simply want to note that even before we were aware of it, SYMBIS and P/E were leveraging this new scientific insight. How? By helping couples gain personal insight into themselves as individuals (heightening self-awareness) and similar insights about their partner (increased understanding). More importantly, debriefing a couple's assessment report also lifts the curtain on the unique chemistry of their relationship—enabling a new and profound sense of mutual empathy that gets at what we are only now beginning to understand at a neurological level. While more study will certainly be conducted, we can assure you that mirror neurons between spouses are firing between them to generate more harmony and stronger bonds.[12]

The News Keeps Getting Better

If you can't tell from this chapter, we are evangelistic about the science of assessments for couples. With assessment scores, it's long been established that we can predict with 85 percent accuracy which couples will separate and divorce within a three-year span.[13] Pretty remarkable. And every year, more studies are published that underscore the clinical value of assessments and help us refine the instruments. Every year we discover ways to improve tactics for our facilitators.

But we feel compelled to leave you in this chapter with one more thought that makes their usefulness unmistakable. It comes from a study that has stunned more than a few skeptical scholars. The study involved clergy and counselors offering the PREPARE assessment[14] to engaged couples and consisted of three groups: (1) a control group that did not take the assessment or meet with a facilitator, (2) a group that took the assessment but did not receive feedback, and (3) a group who took the assessment and received four feedback sessions with a facilitator.[15]

The hypothesis is what you would guess. We believed that premarital couples would benefit most from taking the assessment and receiving feedback and less so from just taking the assessment.

> *Mutual empathy is the great unsung human gift.*
>
> —Jean Baker Miller

With 153 couples, all less than two months away from marriage, the groups were formed randomly and ensured no significant differences between the couples in terms of age, years knowing their partner, education, income, ethnicity, and so on. The same care was taken to ensure that the facilitators (70 percent clergy and 30 percent counselors) received no special or additional training in PREPARE, other than the standard one-day workshop.

Not surprisingly, the two groups of couples who experienced the assessment, with and without the feedback, showed significant improvement over the control group for more than 90 percent of the couples. They performed better in communication, conflict management, intimacy, and so on. We expected these results based on numerous earlier studies.

What surprised us, however, was that the group who experienced the assessment alone, without any feedback, demonstrated significant improvement too. In other words, just answering the questions on the inventory, without debriefing the results with a facilitator, resulted in overall improvement. While not as high as the group who received debriefing sessions with a facilitator, these couples had measurable improvement—a 30 percent increase in positive couple scores—and reported the experience to be helpful to their relationship.

How could this be? How could simply answering questions individually improve satisfaction in the relationship and increase aptitude in areas that bode well for success? Most likely, the experience simply served as a catalyst for conversation about their own relationship. "How did you answer those questions about in-laws?" It simply got them talking about topics that they may have neglected.

So imagine the value you bring to the discussion couples are already motivated to have. The energy and engagement of a sound assessment along with your guidance and expertise are the best chance a couple has to learn the rudiments of lasting love. Especially when you understand the typology of couples, as we are about to see in the next chapter.

4

EVERY MARRIAGE
IS UNIQUE

There is little difference in people, but that
little difference makes a big difference.
—*W. Clement Stone*

Every autumn semester for many years running, we (Les and Leslie) have taught a university class called Personality. You'll find this course in every undergraduate curriculum in colleges in the country. It's a standard requirement for psychology majors. Scholars agree that this information is essential to a basic education in the science of psychology.

We've come to believe that this information should also be required study for anyone who gets married. Why? Because our personalities determine the very essence of who we are and why each of us does what we do.

It all begins in our DNA—that molecule found in almost every cell of our bodies. It not only encodes the basic blueprint for our biological traits and predispositions, but it also includes much of the encoding for the basics in our unique personalities—our patterns of thinking, feeling, and behaving.[1] And our personalities play a central role in our love lives. Personality traits, for example, shape how we communicate and how we like someone to communicate with us. Personality shapes how we give and receive affection, whether we tend to show up early or late, and whether we like routine or variety. In short, couples love the way they do, in great part, because of their genetic disposition.

Allow us to say it another way: Your genes, along with the environment you were raised in, shape your desire to give and receive love in particular ways.[2] And when two people marry, combining their individual genetic makeups, personality differences are inevitable.[3] No husband and wife, no matter how much they have in common, ever have the same personality. Some of the personality differences are clearly evident. Some are so subtle, they can baffle even the most astute of couples, leaving them scratching their heads:

"Why would he say that?" a flustered wife wonders.

"How could she feel that way?" a confused husband questions.

Now here's the surprising fact: Humans share about 99.9 percent of their DNA. This means that only 0.1 percent of each person's DNA is unique.[4] Whether you hail from Algeria or Argentina, Zaire or Zimbabwe, your genetic makeup is strikingly similar to that of every other person on earth. Your genome and everyone else's are 99.9 percent identical. In the famed double helix of our two intertwined DNA strands, only a very small fraction makes us unique from one another. That small fraction contains three billion pairs of nucleotides, or chemical bases of genetic information, we inherit from our moms and dads. And that minuscule proportion is enough to create seeming chasms of dissimilarity, causing consternation, as well as excitement, for every married couple. Why? Because personalities determine what we say and when we say it, what we do or don't do, and why we do or say anything at all.

> *All weddings are similar, but every marriage is different.*
>
> —John Berger

It's tough to comprehend. Think of it this way. There are more than three million differences between your genome and anyone else's. And it's these three million different sources of genetic information that make your personality exceptional.

Of course, the same holds true for your spouse. Your marriage brings together two completely unique and special personalities. There has never been a combination like you two before. In all human history, marriage has never witnessed your inimitable combinations of personalities. Your relationship is unprecedented. It is unmatched. There's never been a marriage exactly like yours before.

> *Do not free a camel of the burden of his hump; you may be freeing him from being a camel.*
>
> —G. K. Chesterton

That's why you may have found that what seems to work wonders for another couple doesn't seem to help the two of you much at all. And in your therapeutic work with couples you've undoubtedly found that a technique or exercise that's perfect for one couple seems to fall flat with another. This chapter will help you understand why, and more importantly, what to do about it.

Every couple is unique. It's what caused German poet Heinrich Heine to liken marriage to "the high sea for which no compass has yet been invented!" Sure, there are universal techniques and strategies that can help nearly every couple. Empathy is a good example. What married relationship couldn't benefit from more of that? But putting a technique or strategy for more empathy into practice for each couple becomes a challenge that hinges on that couple's combined personalities.

That's why we dedicate this chapter to understanding the unquestionable importance of personality. More specifically, we want to provide you with the most salient elements of this science so that you can further apply it to the interventions you use with the couples in your care.

The Dynamic Interplay of Two Personalities

Of course, we can't x-ray a personality, but we *can* observe it. Why? Because our personalities are evident in our behaviors. We can deduce something, for example, about a person's temperament when we notice that they do very careful research before buying a camera. And we can deduce something about personality when we see someone purchase an expensive pair of sneakers on impulse. Our behaviors reveal our personalities. And as Yogi Berra so famously said, "You can observe a lot just by watching." Especially when that "watching" is done around the clock in a marriage.

> *The things that make me different are the things that make me.*
>
> —A. A. Milne

But even with all that watching, spouses don't actually perceive their partner's personality accurately. After all, a great deal of personality is only found on the interior of who we are. That's why, in both SYMBIS and P/E, we go to great lengths to capture an accurate snapshot of each personality and show how they best interact. Not only does this help couples avoid needless friction and frustration, but it elevates the level of harmony and connection.

The first personality measures date back to the eighteenth

century, when personality was assessed through "reading" bumps on the human skull (known as phrenology). We've come a long way since then. Today there are numerous proven models and means for uncovering personality. Both P/E and SYMBIS use two of the most highly regarded and the most thoroughly researched models. P/E, for example, relies on the Five Factor Model of personality which is derived from a statistical analysis of descriptors identifying the core factors of personality.[5] The SYMBIS Assessment depicts the relationship of two personalities on a pinwheel fueled by the decades of research around the DiSC model.[6]

You can readily see that there are eight different spouse types around the pinwheel: Pioneering, Energizing, Affirming,

and so on. But we want you to also take note of the two inner circles of the pinwheel. One has to do with *pace* (fast or slow), and the other has to do with *focus* (task or people).[7]

Task-Oriented versus People-Oriented

Research reveals that all of us fall somewhere along this continuum:

Task-Oriented   **People-Oriented**

| 5 | 4 | 3 | 2 | 1 | 0 | 1 | 2 | 3 | 4 | 5 |

Those who land near the task-oriented end of the continuum prize getting things done. They love an assignment and live by a to-do list. They're gratified by accomplishment, and they stay on task. They're competitive and you can count on them to get a job done. In fact, their task takes priority over other considerations (including their spouse's feelings). Anything that stands in their way of getting the task accomplished will likely become a "distraction." They like to measure their progress. Plainly put, they like to be productive. In the pinwheel model of SYMBIS, the Achieving Spouse is the epitome of this orientation.

Those who land near the people-oriented end of the continuum generally value the emotional wellbeing of others over productivity. They're friendly and good at working with people. They get a "feeling" early on in a conversation and seem to know just what to say. They're rarely forceful or domineering. They're flexible and adapt easily to other people's situations and attitudes. They prize consensus and harmony. They're a team player. In short, they're a people person, and the Cooperative Spouse is most fully in this category.

Slow-Paced versus Fast-Paced

Research also reveals that all of us fall somewhere along this continuum:

Slow-Paced   **Fast-Paced**

5	4	3	2	1	0	1	2	3	4	5

Those who land near the fast-paced end of the continuum live with urgency. They like to get things done *yesterday*! They're ready to get going and don't want to waste time. They love efficiency and want to use their time wisely. They measure success in relationship to speed. They can become impatient more easily than others because their days are packed. They tend to schedule things back to back. Others are often amazed by how they can get so much done in such a short time. They run on rocket fuel and are exemplified in the Achieving Spouse.

If, on the other hand, one is on the slow-paced end of the continuum, they don't overschedule. They like to linger. If they don't get something done today, they'll get it done tomorrow—or the next day. No great rush. They don't let the clock run their life. They move more deliberately than others. They take time to ponder and muse. They are measured and unhurried. These are the common traits of the Deliberating Spouse.

Keep in mind that one type is not better than another. And a person may have qualities from both sides of the continuum; for example, the Deliberating Spouse is squarely slow-paced but in between task-oriented and people-oriented.

Self-insight becomes a given when you help a person discover how they are hardwired. But even more amazing is showing a couple how their two unique personalities mesh. You can literally map it out for them on an assessment report. And by doing so you enable them to see how the combination of their two personalities impacts everything from decision making to problem solving, from managing time to managing money.

> *Always remember that you are absolutely unique. Just like everyone else.*
>
> —Margaret Mead

Say it often: No two marriages are exactly alike. Every marriage is unique. And the more you help a couple discover their personalities' unique dance steps in marriage, the less they'll step on one another's toes. Not only that, you'll enable them, as you're about to see, to reach the highest levels of happiness and fulfillment—what we call becoming a *vitalized* couple.

The Five Types of Married Couples

Mixing two personalities together in marriage is not the only distinction that makes each couple unique. You can also factor in a typology or a measure of interpersonal health. Obviously, not every couple is at the same level of functioning. Couples vary in levels of happiness together. If you've seen more than just a handful of marriages in your work as a marriage champion, you know that it's not unusual for one partner to be much happier than the other. Research reveals a low correla-

The goal in marriage is not to think alike, but to think together.

—Robert C. Dodds

tion in marital satisfaction between spouses. In other words, if you know the satisfaction level of one marriage partner, you will only be able to predict the other partner's marital satisfaction 25 percent of the time.[8]

To identify the differences between happy and unhappy couples, I (David), along with colleagues, conducted a national study with over fifty thousand married couples. Based on their satisfaction scores, we classified 20,675 couples as "happily married," and 20,590 as "unhappily married." The middle group of about ten thousand couples were not included in the two groups because their satisfaction scores were either moderate or one partner was high and one was low.

Through in-depth analysis using the ENRICH assessment, five patterns or "types" of couples emerged, ranging from very happy couples to the most unhappy:

Vitalized Couples

The happiest couple type, these couples have strengths in most aspects of their relationships, including communication, conflict resolution, finances, and their sexual relationship. Eighteen percent of all couples fall into this category, and only 14 percent of individuals in vitalized marriages have ever considered divorce. Vitalized couples enjoy deep understanding and mutual respect. They've found the path to lasting love.

Harmonious Couples

These couples are very happy and have many strengths, but not as many strengths as Vitalized couples. They are satisfied with most areas of their marriage. Twenty-four percent of all married couples fall into this category, and only 28 percent of the individuals in Harmonious marriages have ever considered divorce. Harmonious couples prioritize their relationship, share chores around the house, and do pretty well on deciding how to spend their money. They are particularly satisfied when it comes to how they've learned to resolve conflict together.

Conventional Couples

These couples are generally happy and are "conventional" because they have more strengths in traditional areas, including agreement on spiritual beliefs, agreement on traditional roles, and a strong, supportive network of family and friends. However, they have lower scores in areas involving more internal dynamics, such as communication, conflict resolution, and personality compatibility. Seventeen percent of all married couples fall into this category, and 37 percent of them have considered divorce. These couples are somewhat happy together, but they sometimes feel isolated from each other even though they may enjoy times together in their social circle with friends and family. This marriage looks better from the outside than it really is. They don't discuss their relationship much because it so often stirs up conflict and communication problems.

Conflicted Couples

These couples are unhappy. They contend with unresolved issues, and they disagree in many areas of their relationship. They have especially low scores in communication and conflict resolution, which only exacerbates the feeling of being at odds. When the infatuation fades, as you might guess, these couples are the most likely to seek marriage therapy. Twenty-two percent of all couples are in this category, and 73 percent of individuals in this group have considered divorce.

Devitalized Couples

These couples are very unhappy. They live as distant roommates, and the stress in their home is palpable. In fact, they go out of their way to avoid each other. They've been worn down by perpetual conflict, and avoidance is now their mode. They function separately and feel isolated. While they may have had strengths earlier in their relationship, almost all aspects of their relationship are now a challenge. Nineteen percent of all couples fall into this category, and 90 percent of the individuals in these relationships have considered divorce.

This typology of marriages, these five categories, can help you pinpoint the kinds of couples you are working with. It can help you zero in on what needs to change or improve for couples in each category. It can also serve as an aspirational framework in helping your couples climb to the next level. And keep this insight handy to share: *Unlike personality, the couple type that fits the couple in your counseling office does not have to forever define them.* It's simply how they are *today*. Awareness creates intention. And there's a direct correlation between deliberate actions and positive outcomes. Proven programs, like P/E and SYMBIS, have helped countless couples make progress and move into the categories where they can enjoy more happiness together.

Opposites Attract?

You've heard it before. But it's not true. Opposites don't attract. We're attracted to people who are most like us (especially when it comes to our values). It just turns out that no matter how much you have in common, it often feels like you married your opposite. Relative to each other, one of you is an early riser, for example. By comparison, the other is a night owl. Voila! Your opposite. Truth be told, when opposites truly do attract, they soon attack. People generally marry other people who share their values and are most like them. "Birds of a feather," at least in marriage, "flock together."

In fact, researchers find that the longer we are married, we even meld our personality traits and begin to look more like one another. You've probably heard this as a folktale (not to mention resembling our pets), but some research backs it up. Over time, studies show, married couples begin to look more alike because they share emotions so often that they experience the same "subtle shifts in facial wrinkles and other facial contours," according to a University of Michigan study.[9] Laughing at the same TV shows and furrowing your brow at the same rambunctious kid, for example, bring on similarities.

> *A long marriage is two people trying to dance a duet and two solos at the same time.*
>
> —Anne Taylor Fleming

They report that couples who originally bore no particular resemblance to each other when first married had, after twenty-five years of marriage, though subtle, come to look more alike. Moreover, researchers say the more marital happiness a couple reported, the greater their increase in facial resemblance.

Regardless of how accurate or relevant this intriguing finding might be, one thing is certain: *Couples who study each other's personalities—whether they are similar or dramatically different—and work on proven skills for a deeper connection are the most likely to enjoy harmonious and vital relationships.* These are the couples, as we'll see in the next chapter, who have discovered the keys to heartfelt intimacy.

5

INTIMACY REQUIRES TWO KEYS

To keep a lamp burning, we have
to keep putting oil in it.
—*Mother Teresa*

As a professor at Yale, Robert Sternberg studied romantic love long before it was fashionable with scholars. In his groundbreaking project he discovered love's essential ingredients: passion, commitment, and intimacy.[1] Passion is physical. Commitment is willful. And intimacy is emotional. Of the three ingredients, intimacy, the focus of this chapter, is the number one predictor of happiness—or unhappiness—in marriage.

An intimacy deficit is toxic for couples. It wreaks havoc in a relationship. You've seen it in your counseling office. Communication breaks down. Conflicts erupt. Marriage champions, including professional therapists, say it is often the most challenging issue they face with couples.[2]

Look up *intimacy* in a dictionary and you'll see words like *close*, *warm*, *familiar*, *affectionate*, *caring*, and *understanding*. Some researchers say that intimacy emerges when you see less "me" and "you" in the relationship and more "we" and "us."[3] It engenders interdependence, a detailed knowledge of each other, and a deep sense of belonging.[4] "You understand me and I understand you like nobody on the planet." That's the feeling of intimacy. It's a feeling of being best friends.[5] And it's what separates happy, harmonious, and vitalized couples from unhappy, conflicted, and devitalized couples.

An important 2004 study found intimacy to involve two criteria.[6] First, intimate partners *share information*. They have secrets, inside jokes, and information about each other that nobody else knows. Second, intimate partners not only share information, they have a *deep understanding of each other*. This allows them to know each other's thoughts, habits, inclinations, and preferences. Elsa Einstein, wife of Albert, was once asked if she understood her husband's theory of relativity. "No," she said, "but I know how he likes his tea." That's part of emotional intimacy.

Marriage is the closest bond possible between two people. Legally, socially, emotionally, physically, there is no other means of getting closer to another human being. We long to belong to another person who knows us and loves us like nobody else. Intimacy is the rocket fuel of marriage, and it enables couples to transcend themselves to explore the universe of love together.

> A good marriage isn't something you find; it's something you make, and you have to keep on making it.
>
> —Gary Thomas

Eventually, however, couples also discover that such closeness can be constricting. It pulls our very identity into the vortex of another human life, sometimes leaving little room to breathe. Intimacy can leave nowhere to hide. It shines a light on our dark side. And does anyone, really, want to be known *that* well? Who wants to live under surveillance?

Yet this is the tradeoff. Intimacy brings with it the best conversations of our lives. And when conflict emerges, as it always does, that same intimacy can be wielded like a steely blade. If the scuffle gets bad enough, secrets confessed in confidence are used to cut the connective tissues between partners. Truth is, intimacy is a double-edged sword. It can be used to open up incredibly deep levels of communication, but, given time and enough unhealthy conflict, it can also cut the very heart out of a once loving relationship.

Good communication is as stimulating as black coffee.

—Anne Morrow Lindbergh

Intimacy is the most powerful predictor of satisfaction and happiness in marriage. That's why we devote this chapter to the science of intimacy. More specifically, we focus on two factors that make lasting intimacy possible: communication and conflict management. As you're about to see, good communication skills are the number one predictor of success in marriage while poor conflict skills are the number one predictor of divorce.[7] If we are ever to help couples enjoy lasting love and enduring intimacy, it will be because we help them improve their communication and better manage their conflicts. Communication and conflict management are the two keys to deeper intimacy.

How to Say What You Mean and Understand What You Hear

Terri Orbuch at the University of Michigan, along with her colleagues, has studied the same 373 couples for almost three decades. Among her findings in this longitudinal study, she's come up with a prescription for increasing emotional intimacy: ten minutes a day of quality conversation.[8] That's it.

"Many couples think they're communicating with each other when they sort out who will pick up the kids, pay the bills or call the grandparents," says Orbuch. But that's not the kind of communication she's talking about. Her research and many others consistently show a link between happy marriages and sharing personal feelings, fears, and doubts.

Why is this important? Because it's long been established that most married couples enjoy open and frequent conversations early on in their relationship, but it typically declines if they are not intentional, especially when kids come along. In other words, as marriages mature, self-disclosure risks leveling off.[9]

> It is terrible to speak well and be wrong.
>
> —Sophocles

So what can you do to help couples keep this from happening? How can you increase the odds that couples will spend at least ten minutes a day in quality conversation? Here are a few proven methods you can use with the couples in your care. Based on research, these are some of the most important steps you can help your couples take.

Establish Emotional Safety

In a P/E study involving fifty thousand married couples, we identified the most problematic issues in couples' communication. The number one complaint: "I wish my partner was more willing to share his or her feelings." Seventy-six percent of couples report having this problem. The solution, of course, is vulnerability. And the onramp to vulnerability is emotional safety.[10] Couples have their best conversations when they both feel emotionally safe.

Psychologist and author Sue Johnson, known for her work on bonding attachments, explains that vulnerability is the primary way to strengthen a marital bond and keep love alive because it creates emotional safety.[11]

Stephen Porges, a pioneer in the field of neuroscience, confirms that we have an imperative for emotional safety deeply wired into our brains.[12] Only if we trust another will we open ourselves in a conversation. So, if a couple is suffering from chronic disconnection, don't make the mistake of thinking you can simply teach them communication techniques and they'll have instant warmth and connection. The problem goes deeper. It's an emotional safety issue. That's the starting place.

In other words, change your emotional state and the words follow. Not the other way around. When people are emotionally disconnected, the use of communication techniques can make them feel manipulated. That's when couples say something like, "I'm validating you more than you're validating me." Communication techniques in the absence of a safe emotional connection feel unnatural ("What I hear you saying . . ."). They feel more suited for a therapist's office than a couple's kitchen or bedroom. In fact, more than one research study revealed that teaching communication skills can increase marital distress.[13] Why? Because, unfortunately, the execution of the technique becomes the goal rather than making a genuine connection.

The solution? Consider helping couples discover their unique "safety needs." What makes one person feel emotionally safe in a relationship will probably not be the very same for their partner. In fact, it never is. For nearly a century, researchers have consistently identified four safety needs that are shaped by our personalities: (1) gaining control of time, (2) winning approval, (3) maintaining loyalty, and (4) archiving quality standards. Each of us has a varying combination of these safety needs.[14] The hardwiring of personality manifests the unique combination of these four. If you're using the SYMBIS Assessment, you'll see exactly how each person stacks up in all of them and how they compare with their spouse. You can also discover more practical applications of these safety needs in our book and his/her workbooks, *Love Talk*.[15]

Don't Neglect the Key to Better Listening

Sixty-five percent of couples agree with this statement: "My partner often does not understand how I feel." In other words, the majority of spouses do not feel listened to. "It is impossible to overemphasize the immense need we have to be really listened to, to be taken seriously, to be understood," said renowned Swiss counselor Paul Tournier. "No one can develop freely in this world and find a full life without feeling understood by at least one person."[16]

> *There are people who, instead of listening to what is being said to them, are already listening to what they are going to say themselves.*
>
> —Albert Guinon

Listening is one of the single most important aspects of communication. The survivability of our conversations depends on it, and yet we too often take it for granted. American psychologist Theodor Reik, one of Freud's earliest and most brilliant students, wrote a book in 1948 called *Listening with the Third Ear*.[17] The title was his way of underscoring the fact that listening is not about hearing words. It's about hearing the message and the feelings behind them. And the most effective and efficient way of doing just that is through empathy. Sure, you can teach couples how to "reflect feelings" and that can be very effective—but only when it comes from a genuine and empathic heart.[18]

We (Les and Leslie) often tell our university counseling students that sympathy is like throwing a life ring into the water to help a struggling person. Empathy, however, is like diving into that water yourself to bring them back to the shore. It's the heroic call of every marriage champion. And it's a skill we can teach couples. Helping them see the world through their spouse's eyes never fails to ease their spirit, draw them closer, and help them listen better.

But there's a catch.

Research reveals that when couples are asked *if* they empathize with each other, they invariably say yes.[19] Okay, fair enough. But when these same couples are asked to "empathize" with characters in a story (while watching a movie, for example), a measure of their emotions reveals that they aren't nearly as good at empathy as they thought they were. In fact, their understanding of the emotions for the characters they were empathizing with is at the same level as those who were instructed *not* to empathize with a character's emotions. Incredible, right?

But here's the part of the study that was even more surprising (and encouraging): With a little more emphasis, a little more explanation, of how to empathize with the characters, the results were significantly improved. Adults who were instructed to "imagine yourself as being the other person" were far more understanding and articulate of what a character was experiencing. In other words, just a tiny bit of help dramatically improved their capacity for empathy. Keep that in mind the next time you are helping a couple communicate. A little help with empathy can go a long way.[20]

So we'll say it again: Listening requires the intentional effort to consciously see the world from the partner's point of view. It's an action that will never fail to ease their spirits and will almost always draw them closer together. That's the value of learning to listen with your third ear.

Fighting the Good Fight

Not all fights are created equal. A "good fight," in contrast to a "bad fight," is helpful, not hurtful. It's positive, not negative. In a good fight, partners are allies, not adversaries. A good fight stays clean while a bad fight gets dirty.[21] And 93 percent of couples who fight dirty will be divorced in ten years, according to researchers at the University of Utah.[22] Another study at Ohio State University showed that unhealthy marital arguments contribute significantly to a higher risk of heart attacks, headaches, back pain, and a whole slew of problems—not to mention unhappiness.[23] In the end, bad fights lead to marriages that are barely breathing and eventually die. In fact, researchers can now predict with more than 90 percent accuracy whether a couple will stay together or not based solely on *how* they fight.[24] Not *whether* they fight, but *how* they fight.

More studies on conflict have been conducted than any other topic related to marriage. A mountain of scientific research exists on this subject. The remaining portion of this chapter is not in any way exhaustive, but it's valuable. And we begin with one of the most acclaimed research projects on marriage of our time.

What to Avoid

A few steps from our offices in Seattle, you can cross a canal that joins Puget Sound to Lake Washington and walk down a trail that will take you to the University of Washington. It's on this campus that some of the most groundbreaking research on marriage has ever been conducted.

In 1986, researcher and clinician John Gottman founded a research laboratory, the Love Lab, with funding from the NIMH where he used video, heart rate monitors, and measures of pulse amplitude to code the behavior and physiology of hundreds of couples at different points in their relationship. He's done more yeoman work on conflict in marriage than anyone we know.

> *The most important thing in communication is to hear what isn't being said.*
>
> —Peter F. Drucker

Over lunch one day at a picturesque restaurant between our two campuses, we (Les and Leslie) asked John how he predicts the end of a marriage. That's when we first learned about what he calls the Four Horsemen of the Apocalypse, a metaphor from the New Testament depicting the end of times. But in this case, they signify doom for a marriage. So much so that he's been able to predict with more than 90 percent accuracy whether a couple will succeed or fail in their marriage based solely on the presence of these four horsemen in their communication.[25]

> *A good listener is a good talker with a sore throat.*
>
> —Katharine Whitehorn

Identifying the four caution flags is a necessary first step to eliminating them and replacing them with healthy counterparts.[26] You may have already studied them, but they're worthy of a quick review so that you can improve your focus on them and better explore them with the couples in your care.

Criticism

Every fight begins with a critical comment. "You always make us late," for example. Criticizing your partner is different than offering a critique or voicing a complaint. It's an attack. In his book *Why Marriages Succeed or Fail*, Gottman points out that complaints attack a situation that can be improved.[27] Nothing wrong with that. Complaining keeps us honest and authentic. Criticism, on the other hand, attacks the person: "You never pick up your clothes." When you complain, you don't blame. But when you criticize, you attack the person's character. So when you help couples learn how to turn criticisms into complaints, you're making a world of difference.

Contempt

That day over lunch, we asked John what single quality was most detrimental to a couple's wellbeing. Dr. Gottman didn't have to think twice. "It's contempt," he said. "Contempt is so lethal to love that it ought to be outlawed." He went on to tell us how predictive contempt is of turmoil and eventual divorce for couples. Contempt is any belittling remark that makes your spouse feel about an inch tall. It's often sarcastic, caustic, mocking, and downright mean. In fact, it doesn't even have to be spoken. It can happen when a spouse rolls their eyes at their partner. Contempt conveys disdain, disapproval, and dishonor. In short, contempt conveys disrespect. You need to help couples avoid contempt like they avoid poison.

Defensiveness

This third horseman is typically a response to criticism—and it's nearly omnipresent when a marriage is on the rocks. It's self-protective armor we put on in the form of righteous indignation or innocent victimhood in an attempt to ward off a perceived threat. And it's almost never successful. Excuses just tell a partner that they're not taken seriously, which perpetuates the tension and sometimes propels it into high gear. That's why effective marriage champions help couples learn to make a habit of setting aside their defensive armor.

Stonewalling

Typically a response to contempt, this horseman occurs when a partner withdraws from the interaction, shuts down, or simply stops responding. Rather than confronting the issues with their partner, the stonewaller makes evasive maneuvers such as tuning out, turning away, acting busy, or engaging in distracting behaviors. Unfortunately, stonewalling isn't easy to stop. It's the result of feeling *physiologically flooded*, Gottman's term for the emotional hijacking of your brain, making productive communication next to impossible. By the way, men stonewall quicker than women, while women get to criticism faster than men. Read on to learn how to combat this one.

There you have it, four behaviors to stay clear of—to avoid

at all costs—if you want to have a good fight. But on the other side of the proverbial coin, research reveals four behaviors we can help couples pursue to counteract and replace these harmful horsemen.

What to Pursue

When we (Les and Leslie) were combing through hundreds of scholarly studies for our book *The Good Fight*, we wanted to identify the basic elements that characterize a healthy conflict. With countless journal articles spread out on the floor of our office, we tried to categorize them and came up with four critical elements—the essentials. They're easy to remember because, in fact, they spell CORE: Cooperation, Ownership, Respect, and Empathy.

Cooperation—Good Fighters Fight for a Win-Win

A study reported in *Psychological Science* discovered that the "best" arguer in a couple is the one who works in tandem with their partner. According to the study, the person who says "we" the most during an argument suggests the best solutions. Researchers from the University of Pennsylvania and the University of North Carolina at Chapel Hill, in a study with fifty-nine couples, found that spouses who used second-person pronouns (you) tended toward negativity in interactions. Those making use of first-person plural pronouns (we) provided positive solutions to problems. The study concluded: "'We' users may have a sense of shared interest that sparks compromise and other ideas pleasing to both partners. 'You'-sayers, on the contrary, tend to criticize, disagree, justify, and otherwise [teem] with negativity."[28]

The key to cooperation, of course, is found in reframing a conflict from "win-lose" to "win-win." Healthy conflict is not a competition. Marriage is not a zero-sum game. Win-win is a frame of mind that seeks mutual benefit. It's an attitude that says, "If you win, I win too."

But let's be honest. Not every dispute has a solution for both sides. Julie and John Gottman report that an astounding 69 percent of relationship problems are perpetual. "Perpetual problems exist even in the healthiest of relationships due to lasting personality differences between partners," Gottman states. These problems don't have a solution and are therefore not going to get "fixed."[29] On a bulletin board in our kitchen is a cartoon that depicts a cat and a dog standing in front of a judge's bench. The dog is saying: "Let's agree to disagree." When a win-win can't be found, it's time to do just that—agree to disagree.

> *The course of true love never did run smooth.*
>
> —Shakespeare

Ownership—Good Fighters Own Their Piece of the Pie

Self-centered pride is at the heart of every bad fight. Research shows that when pride sets in, a partner will continue an argument 34 percent of the time even if they know they're wrong—or can't remember what the fight was about. And a full 74 percent will fight on even if they feel "it's a losing battle."[30]

Maybe you've seen the bumper sticker: "The man who can smile when things are going badly has just thought of someone to blame it on." Sadly, this is sometimes not too far from the truth when it comes to conflict and couples. It's so tempting to play the blame game. Why? Because we think it will let us off the hook.

In social psychology, there is a phenomenon called *fundamental attribution error*. In plain language, it means when someone is behaving in a way we don't like, we tend to attribute their behavior to ill will rather than bad circumstances. Let's say your partner is late for dinner. Research shows that you're more likely to think, "They don't care" than "Traffic must have been awful."

When we blame our spouse (or anything else), we shift responsibility. We think our fancy footwork puts us in the clear. Of course, it doesn't. Blame only exacerbates a bad fight. But in a good fight, the fighters own up. How? We've literally drawn a circle on a piece of paper in a couple's counseling session and said, "This is a pie that represents all the chaos in your marriage. Now, 100 percent of the blame is in that pie, because that's where all the chaos is." We then give each a pen and say, "Draw a slice of pie that you think represents your responsibility for the chaos." Amazingly simple—and effective.

Respect—Good Fighters Steer Clear of Belittling

Everyone wants respect. Scratch that. We *need* respect. We can't have a relationship without it. An attitude of respect builds a bridge of trust between a husband and wife even when they are feeling at odds. It's the exact opposite of what Gottman describes as contempt. Respect does more than curb contempt, however. It helps us listen before speaking. It drives us to understand before passing judgment. And when we're wounded, respect sets the stage for forgiveness.[31] I (Les), along with Everett Worthington at Virginia Commonwealth

University, conducted several studies investigating forgiveness as a clinical method with couples and found that respect reduces the "injustice gaps" in a relationship, making forgiveness more likely.[32]

Empathy—Good Fighters Step into Each Other's Shoes

We've already talked about empathy, but the research here compels a quick callback. If you want to instantly and dramatically increase the odds of experiencing a good fight, you may only need to put this single core quality of empathy into practice. Why? Because research shows that as much as 90 percent of marital spats can be resolved if all the couple does is accurately see the issue from each other's perspective.[33] Don't miss this point: nine times out of ten, conflicts may be resolved when couples step into each other's shoes. Enough said.

> *Conflict is inevitable, but combat is optional.*
>
> —Max Lucado

The more readily you can draw on these elements of a bad fight, the four horsemen, and replace them with the CORE of a good fight, the better you'll be able to help those couples in your care. Every marriage can benefit from learning the four things to avoid and the four things to proactively pursue. In the next chapter we delve into what science has to say about the way our families of origin forever shape our marriages.

6

FAMILY TIES PULL STRINGS

If you cannot get rid of the family skeleton,
you may as well make it dance.
—*George Bernard Shaw*

One of my first counseling clients was an exhibitionist. That's right. The kind that wears a trench coat, surreptitiously sneaks up on unsuspecting women, and flashes them. This guy, we'll call him Randy, got off on the reactive shock of exposing his genitals to strangers. And it wasn't an isolated incident. Randy had a compulsive pattern of "indecent exposure." He'd been caught twice by the campus police at Penn State.

On the third incident, they sent him to me for treatment. I (David) was still a doctoral student under clinical supervision in the campus clinic. Steeply trained in person-centered therapy, the nonprescriptive Rogerian approach to counseling, I met with Randy and mustered all the "unconditional positive regard" and patient understanding of his compulsion that I could. When it came to getting Randy to talk, it was easy. He wasn't shy (no big surprise). In fact, he was verbose. But we didn't seem to be making much progress.

After a few sessions, I was talking in a supervision meeting about my struggle to help Randy. That's when a fellow doctoral student, Craig Jones, spoke up: "I've got a client that's a tough one too." Craig went on to describe a young woman, we'll call her Carol, who was suffering from extreme snake phobia. Granted, there weren't many literal snakes slithering around the bustling campus of Penn State, but that didn't hinder her irrational fear. In fact, it had become debilitating. Carol needed every drawer in a desk or dresser to be opened and checked for snakes before she could enter a room. You can imagine how this hampered her life.

Craig, like me and every other student in our counseling program, was practicing the Rogerian methods to help his client, but progress was slow. After the clinical supervision meeting, Craig and I were chatting and came up with a thought. "What if we had both of our clients together in the same room with us?" one of us mused. "That's an interesting thought."

> *Whoever said that death and taxes are the only inevitable things in life was overlooking an obvious third one: family.*
>
> —William J. Doherty

So we brought the idea to our supervisor. He immediately shut the idea down: "It's not done. Give the Rogerian principles time to work."

"You do person-centered group therapy," Craig countered. "This would just be like that."

"What do you mean?"

"Well," Craig continued, "David and I would be doing group therapy with two clients—that's four people. A group."

"You've got me there," our supervisor said. "Try it."

So, we did. The next week we made arrangements for both Randy and Carol to meet with us in a counseling office. Little did we know, however, that they were married. No kidding. Randy and Carol were a married couple. Surprised? Of course. We had no idea. So, as it turned out, Craig and I were beginning the first couple's counseling session we'd ever heard of. Nobody was doing that. The concept was never discussed.

There were no books on marriage therapy. But that's what we were doing.

And guess what? It was working. We didn't talk about the symptoms of either one of them. Not a peep about exhibitionism or snake phobia. We simply got the two of them talking about their feelings and their families. But that wasn't as easy as it sounds. Every time Randy began to open up, Carol would interrupt and derail the conversation. In fact, after a couple of sessions of watching her interrupt Randy, I said something that would have made Carl Rogers wince: "Carol, if you interrupt Randy one more time, I'm going to move your chair over to the corner of the room and you won't be able to talk until you're asked to do so."

Talk about a shakeup! I half expected our supervisor, who was observing through a mirror, to burst through the door and immediately kick me out of the counseling profession. But he didn't. The session continued. Randy and Carol began talking, really talking. We gave them a few tips or skills for better conversations with each other. Again, no discussion of symptoms, just the dynamic of their relationship, the homes they grew up in, and their feelings about all of it. Progress was being made. They told us they were enjoying physical intimacy like never before. They were both feeling understood in new ways. Something good was happening for this couple.

By the fourth session together, Randy reported something surprising: "You won't believe this," he told us. "This week I haven't had to go into our apartment first to check the drawers for snakes." He told us that Carol was barely talking about snakes anymore. Interestingly, compulsive flashing wasn't an issue either.

What just happened? Craig and I, along with our supervisor, asked ourselves this question more than once following that session. In fact, personally, I couldn't shake the question. I was more than intrigued. I had to know. Therapeutic magic seemed to occur by seeing a husband and wife together in counseling. *Why hadn't this been done before? Why wasn't it being taught?*

> *The shadow cast by the family tree is truly an astonishingly long one.*
>
> —Maggie Scarf

These questions and a hundred others became a pivot point in my studies. I wanted to learn more. When I looked for a program that would encourage this kind of treatment with couples, the only funded program in existence was at the University of Minnesota. That's where they were seeing couples and even entire families together in counseling. So that's where I headed for a postdoctoral fellowship in something they were calling "marriage and family therapy." Little did I know how this would be instrumental in developing a model for researching and treating couples in a way that had never been done before.

That's why we dedicate this chapter to helping you understand and apply the science behind *systems*—"a group of interacting entities that form a unified whole." More specifically, *family systems* and the practical application of what has come to be called the Circumplex Model. If this sounds mysterious or complicated, it's not. Stay with us and you'll see how it can be revolutionary for many of the couples in your care.

What's a Family System?

Albert Einstein, of course, is best known for his theory of relativity. It revolutionized scientific thought and made matter and energy no longer distinct but exchangeable. He found power in relationships within the cosmos. Einstein and other physicists proved that each person is a representation of the whole and that each profoundly affects the system as a whole. Einstein and scientists who followed him demonstrated that the elements of the stars are in our bones, that we are more energy than mass, more process than "stuff," and that we are all mutually influenced by all humankind.

This view of connectedness becomes the lens for looking at marriage and family therapy. The family is a system pulsing with energy. "You know how when you put your hand on something like a radio that is plugged in and you can feel the energy going through it?" asks neuropsychologist Paul Pearsall. "That's like our family. You can feel our energy when we're together."[1] And that's the crux of a family system, interacting components mutually affecting one another. This idea was new in the early 1970s. Up until then, therapists looked at dysfunction as an individual problem, not a systemic family problem. In fact, a pioneering band of maverick psychiatrists were plowing ground for this

It is in the family that patterns of emotional reactivity develop and interpersonal relationships are established that pattern and color all subsequent relationships.

—Theodor Lidz

new field at the NIMH, and chief among them was Murray Bowen. He and other colleagues observed how couples and families functioned upon learning that a family member was diagnosed with schizophrenia.[2]

Their observations focused on how a dramatic diagnosis of schizophrenia affected the entire family. One of their observations: a patient's symptoms are maintained by the family system. This led to the formation of concepts like the *facade of family harmony* and the *double bind* where a person receives two contradictory and rigid messages at the same time, making them unable to follow both. For example, a child might be told by a father, "Always stand up for your rights, no matter who, no matter what!" But that child is also told by the father, "Never question my authority. I am your father and what I say goes!" Such contradictions provide fertile soil for maladjustment. And it led Murray Bowen to study concepts like *differentiation*, where a family member becomes more independent and less dysfunctional.

As fate would have it, I (David) happened to be working just steps away, literally across the street, from Bowen while I was codirecting a longitudinal study of early marriage and family development at the NIMH. In a sense, this area in Bethesda became an epicenter for new thinking and new science around the family system. In fact, family therapy was having an explosive impact on the mental health profession, not only as a technique but as a theoretical approach to treatment. The newly named American Association of Marriage and Family Therapists helped open the way for this new emphasis on the family. They identified three entities to be considered in every relationship: two persons and one couple. In other words, people affect and are affected by their family contexts. Individuals change families, and families change individuals. Even small exchanges between family members have emotional subtexts that can sometimes last a lifetime in the unconscious. The bottom line, and what countless studies have since found, is that everyone's family of origin indelibly shapes them as well as every relationship they ever have, especially their marriage. Family ties pull strings. And one thing we know is that when you get married, you tend to either repeat what you learned in your family or you do the opposite.

> *It is only when we no longer compulsively need someone that we can have a real relationship with them.*
>
> —Anthony Starr

In 1973, only one journal existed in the field of family counseling; there are now dozens of journals dedicated to this research. When I went to the University of Minnesota for my postdoc, it was the only program I could find. Today there are well over 1,500 training programs in marriage and family therapy.

At the front end of this burgeoning field, before its popularity, while conducting research at the NIMH, I began trying to make sense out of the emerging scientific theories on how family systems work. I was also motivated to understand healthy couples and families, not just dysfunctional ones. The result? I came up with what I called the Circumplex Model or what we now refer to as the Relationship Map.[3]

The Relationship Map

Every marital or family system needs enough *cohesiveness*—togetherness or closeness—to give members a sense of identity and belonging. It also needs enough *adaptability*—flexibility or change—to balance family needs for resilience and stability. Both of these, closeness and flexibility, can be assessed along a continuum. And when combined, each on its own axis, they can literally be plotted on a map:

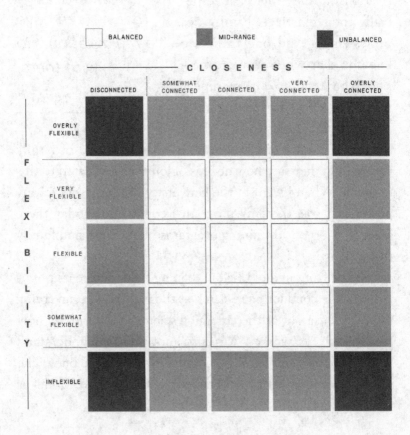

This model, or map, has been used in well over 1,200 scientific studies, making it one of the most highly respected and researched relationship models.[4] It allows practitioners to map couples as well as their families of origin. On its own, the measure is known to social scientists as the *Family Adaptability and Cohesion Evaluation Scales*, or FACES, and has high levels of reliability and validity for discriminating between healthy and unhealthy couples and families.[5] But for marriage champions who are using the P/E assessment, these scales are built into the P/E pages you unpack with a couple, in a simplified version, making it easy to explore.[6] The report contains a Family Map as well as a Couple Map.

As you know from our previous chapter, many studies find that communication and conflict resolution are what distinguishes happy from unhappy couples. But just as important in predicting marital success are a couple's closeness and flexibility.[7] The key to building a healthy relationship in a marriage or a family is to avoid extremes. Balance is the goal. Balanced couples tend to be happier, healthier, and more functional than unbalanced couples who are at the extreme corners of the map.[8] And as you're about to see, a marriage champion can be instrumental in helping couples achieve this.

Understanding Closeness

We know every family needs glue, but not too much and not too little. The poles of this continuum are *enmeshment*, or being "overly connected" at one extreme, and

> *Some people prefer the certainty of misery to the misery of uncertainty.*
>
> —Virginia Satir

disengagement, being "disconnected" at the other. Moderate or balanced levels of closeness are where you find the highest functioning and healthiest relationships. Why? Because it's here that family members are comfortable being alone *and* together. They enjoy harmony in their individuality and their togetherness. Autonomy is respected, and vulnerability is encouraged and appreciated. Members can be honest with their thoughts and feelings, and enjoy quiet—even silence—without secrecy, enabling genuine connection and heartfelt intimacy.

By looking at the extremes and then the balanced, anchored center, the usefulness of this approach with couples becomes abundantly clear.

Disconnected Families

A disconnected relationship is characterized by extreme emotional separateness and little involvement among family members or spouses. Everyone "does their own thing." Secrets abound, and loyalty is tough to detect in these relationships. Nobody seems to feel or feel felt. Vital information is often treated with an air of dispassion: "I thought I told you about the abortion; maybe I didn't." Certain remarks, even monumental ones, are met with dismissive silence. This extreme family system engenders a belief that human beings are basically uncaring and untrustworthy.

Overly Connected Families

At the other end of the connection continuum, the enmeshed relationship has an extreme amount of emotional closeness. Loyalty is demanded. People here behave in ways that close and loving family members *ought* to—and individuation is not acceptable. Genuine closeness is stunted because the members of the system aren't free to be themselves. In this kind of family, it is more important to be who one "should be" than to be who one actually is at the moment. It's all about the group, not the self. Persons are irrationally dependent on each other. Their activities are entangled, and there is little private space. Everybody knows everyone's business. Their energy is focused primarily inside the relationship, with few outside interests or meaningful friendships.

Families with Balanced Connection

Partners in a happy marriage, in the midrange of these two extremes, are more than twice as likely as unhappy couples to find it easy to enjoy doing things together and to ask each other for help. They enjoy a balance of connection.[9] It's in the midrange of connection where couples are most likely to experience what is often referred to as the "love hormone," oxytocin. Studies at Claremont Graduate University have shown that high-oxytocin couples finished each other's sentences, laughed together, and touched each other more often.[10] The chemicals in our body make us easier to love and be loved.[11]

Remember Randy, the exhibitionist, and Carol, his wife with the snake phobia? Where do they land on this continuum? Well, they are what we call "flippers." They flip from one extreme to the other. For example, Carol was overly dependent on Randy to check all the drawers in a room for snakes. And he readily accepted this assignment. They were both operating as enmeshed or "overly connected" in those moments. But once they were settled in at home, they flipped to being "disconnected," each doing their own thing in their own corner of their apartment, barely interacting. Not until after therapy did they begin to live in the midrange between the two extremes, something you can bet wasn't modeled for either of them in their homes growing up.

Striking a Balance with Closeness

The most powerful method a family has of teaching relationship lessons is by example. There's no way around it. We learn how to feel, how to think, and how to act by observing others in our home. And we learn the relationship skills that will either help or hinder the relationships we have as adults.[12] That's why so much can be gained by exploring the role models each person in a marriage grew up with. Stacks of empirical studies make it clear: Helping couples understand the homes they came from is invaluable. Family-of-origin experiences are undisputedly significant influences on marital adjustment.[13]

To be clear, it is normal for couple and family relationships to shift back and forth between togetherness and separateness depending on what is happening in the relationship, but generally speaking, balance is the key. Healthy couples maintain their own individuality *and* their closeness. When it comes to helping couples find a healthy place between the two extremes of being disengaged (too much separation) and enmeshed (too much togetherness), marriage champions can also foster balance with a seemingly simple prescription: a "date night" for married couples. If you're already doing this, keep it up. Research shows that 59 percent of married couples with at least one young child have date night less than once a month—and the positive effect on a relationship requires a date every four weeks.[14]

Any change, even a change for the better, is always accompanied by drawbacks and discomforts.

—Arnold Bennett

If you're wondering if this little prescription makes a difference for couples, wonder no more. A review of the social science literature, including a survey of more than 1,600 married couples, reveals that routine date nights help couples "stay current" with each other's lives and heightens more supportive communication.[15] This is particularly true of couples who have habituated to one another and are beginning to take their relationship for granted, sliding toward disengagement.[16]

In fact, a growing body of research suggests that couples who engage in novel activities that are fun and active, as opposed to the old standby of dinner and a movie, foster an even higher quality of balanced levels of closeness—as long as they choose activities that represent a shared interest of each partner's desires.[17] Not only that, but this novel activity on a date night has also been shown to de-stress the relationship if it's been impacted by work, financial pressure, parenthood, or illness. After a novel date night, levels of irritability and isolation improve.[18]

Another interesting fact on dating for married couples: the odds of divorce for couples who have monthly date nights is 30 percent lower than those who hardly ever go out.[19] How could this be? A study at Utah State University sheds some light. Tom Lee, a professor of marriage and family studies surveyed 1,400 married people. One of the findings was that couples who regularly discuss their long-range plans are more likely to stay happily married. And dreaming about the future as a couple together often happens on a date night. "If you have a long-term view, you realize that the daily ups and downs don't mean as much," he says. "Talking about your shared future communicates, 'I plan on being here.' The message is that there are plenty of good times yet to come."[20]

It's a simple solution that works wonders for balancing levels of closeness for a couple: a once-a-month, novel date night. Of course, dozens of other proven interventions—such as setting boundaries, creating space, cultivating common interests—help to create equilibrium between both separateness and togetherness for couples.

Understanding Flexibility

The strength of a marriage is not dependent on closeness or cohesion alone. It also depends on its ability to adjust to unexpected changes. This requires flexibility with rules, roles, and attitudes. UCLA researcher Allen Parducci posed a simple question: What makes happy couples happy? He found that money, success, health, beauty, intelligence, or power have little to do with a couple's "subjective well-being." Instead, research reveals that the level of a couple's joy is determined by each partner's ability to adjust to things beyond his or her control.[21] Happy and healthy couples flex with life's circumstances. Why does this matter? Because stress is an inevitable part of life. We contend with unexpected injuries, illnesses, financial issues, heartaches, and dramas. Life together demands adaptability— but not too much, and not too little.

Overly Flexible Families

Imagine living in a home that is unpredictable. Parenting is more or less a nightmare. If rules exist, they may change on a whim, just because Dad is in a different mood or out with his buddies. There's no organization, no set place for things. Meals? Don't count on it. Grab a Pop-Tart for breakfast if you can find one. And dinner? You're probably on your own. The kitchen table may have become a workbench with pieces of a motorcycle engine the oldest son is repairing. Mom may be passed out on the couch. Nobody notices much or asks many questions. People come and go. This is life in a family that is overly flexible. Parents offer little leadership. Children's needs may go unmet or at least unnoticed. Chaos is the norm. Dysfunction reigns. The family system is in disarray and lives in a state of confusion and turmoil, like a nation in a state of civil disorder.

Inflexible Families

Instead of having no rules, the inflexible family has nothing but rules—black-and-white rules—designed not only to control actions but the thoughts and feelings of everyone in the system. Often both parents, but sometimes just one, are autocratic. Fear is ever present, just below the surface. And in extreme cases, emotional abuse is common. The home is shipshape, with a place for everything. And if you borrow a tool and don't return it, you'll wish you had. Mealtime may be somber, with only the parents speaking. Children may have gotten the message: don't speak unless spoken to. You won't find much give-and-take in these homes. If you have a differing point of view, say about politics or even what to watch on TV, you'll likely keep it to yourself. Of course, inflexible families don't see themselves as rigid. They'd say they are structured or traditional. They may even have a sense of superiority about how they run their home, the way a military sergeant controls his troops.

Families with Balanced Flexibility

An adaptable or balanced family grows and molds itself to the current needs. It shifts and adjusts to life transitions. This flexibility, in a healthy relationship, also provides a sense of security and support and stability. Partners can almost always count on each other. Consistency encourages confidence and trust in the relationship. In a way, flexibility is like a shock absorber on the relationship. If it's too tight or too loose, the ride is not going to be pleasant. Without flexibility in the relationship, rigid roles make life difficult, especially in times of crisis. And too much flexibility creates chaos.

> *Love is not jealous.*
>
> —1 Corinthians 13:4 NLT

Chaos and rigidity, the two polar opposites of flexibility, engender dysfunction for everyone in the system. So how do Randy and Carol do on this continuum? Again, not too well. While they have rigid roles playing out at times (Randy obeying Carol's demand to cater to her intrusive and irrational fear), they also flip to unexpected impulses and utter chaos and disorder (like Randy exposing himself to women). As with cohesion, the balanced levels of flexibility are the goal; being structured and flexible are more conducive to healthier functioning, while the extremes engender dysfunction.

Striking a Balance with Flexibility

Imagine if you could ask a couple to bring in a file folder of all the lessons they learned from their families of origin. Maybe they'd have a dog-eared journal containing the lesson plans and customized curriculum their parents knowingly and unknowingly used. If you could peruse their personal transcripts, you might discover courses they'd unconsciously taken: "Feelings We Never Talk about in This Family," "The Way We Avoid Arguments," "How We Express and Don't Express Intimacy," "Advanced Blame Shifting," and so on.

It's a fantasy, for sure. But marriage champions can help couples strike a balance when it comes to flexibility by exploring this proverbial file folder. It simply requires intentionality in uncovering family dynamics. As with closeness, you simply need to discuss it. And if you're using the P/E assessment, it conveniently sets you up for the conversation. The Family Map makes it obvious. If a person is nearing the inflexible or rigid extreme, you'll likely find an authoritarian parent who served as a dictator in that person's family. Or maybe you discover a laissez-faire family vibe where rules barely existed. The point is to get to the unspoken rules and unconscious roles we touched on in chapter 1 under "Myths of Marriage" (as it relates to the SYMBIS curriculum). The more you help couples understand the rules and roles they inherited from their families, the more likely they are to make healthier choices when it comes to being flexible in their relationships.[22]

A nice onramp to doing just that is the issue of decision making. Happy couples agree more often than unhappy ones to compromise and make decisions together. In fact, 91 percent of happy couples agree with this statement: "We make most decisions jointly." But only 42 percent of unhappy couples agree with it.[23]

It's become cliché: Marriage is all about compromise. But it's true. And couples living on the polar ends of flexibility never experience compromise. Overly flexible systems acquiesce at the drop of a hat, while inflexible systems don't even entertain the idea of accommodation. Then there's the idea that compromise means both people lose. As comedian Larry David puts it, "A good compromise is when both parties are dissatisfied."

It's a cute joke, but we know there's a better way. And as many can attest, marriage wouldn't survive without it. Whether it's planning a vacation, divvying up household labor, where to spend the holidays, "me time vs. we time," what color to paint the kitchen, deciding what movie to watch, or you name it, marriage is ripe with countless calls for compromise. Unfortunately, for most people compromise conjures up having to accommodate and sacrifice. But numerous studies confirm that's exactly what's required. Nobody said marriage was a cakewalk. It requires working hard to understand your spouse's perspective and adjusting your own desires and expectations in light of them.

Researchers at the Relationship Institute at UCLA conducted a series of studies over a number of years to better understand commitment in marriage and how it affects happiness and longevity of the relationship.[24] Among their findings, they discovered that couples who are willing to compromise are more effective in solving their problems together. Not surprising, right? But the researchers followed these couples for eleven years, interviewing them every six months, and found that of the 172 married couples in the study, all first-time newlyweds, 79 percent were still married. The study's hypothesis was that commitment was the determining factor. But was it? Not according to the couples. Even the couples that ended their marriage still reported being very committed to the relationship. However, they did not exhibit the resolve to sacrifice or work to reach compromises. Compromises, for them, were not part of the commitment. And you guessed it: The happiest of these couples are the ones who stayed committed and were willing to make sacrifices for the sake of the marriage. The researchers pointed out that they didn't "keep score" of how often one person in the partnership got their way. The other couples did.

This is just one in a long list of studies underscoring the value of compromise in building happy and enduring marriages—and how much we need to help couples understand it. At the University of Washington, John Gottman alone has conducted dozens of studies showing similar findings. And he sums it all up by saying, "It is better to bend than to break."

But he also offers some counterintuitive advice: If your goal is to reach a state of compromise, you must first focus on yourself. Define your core needs in the area of your problems, do not relinquish anything that you feel is absolutely essential, and understand that you must be willing to accept your spouse's influence. "You can only be influential if you accept influence," he states. "Compromise never feels perfect. Everyone gains something and everyone loses something. The important thing is feeling understood, respected, and honored in your dreams."[25]

> *Sometimes you'll get so far away from your family you'll think you're outside its influence forever, then before you figure out what's happening, it will be right beside you, pulling the strings.*
>
> —Peter Collier

This may be a tall order, but it's key to helping couples strike a balance between the extremes of rigidity and chaos, between being inflexible and overly flexible.

If you're looking for a practical tool to prescribe to couples, consider a little technique we've used for years. We call it the Conflict Card. It helps couples rate the depth of their discrepancy so they can more readily come to a compromise. Whatever the issue, like how long the in-laws are staying, they choose which number best represents where they are:

1. *I'm not enthusiastic, but it's no big deal to me.*
2. *I don't see it the way you do, but I may be wrong.*
3. *I don't agree, but I can live with it.*
4. *I don't agree, but I'll let you have your way.*
5. *I don't agree and cannot remain silent on this.*
6. *I do not approve, and I need more time.*
7. *I strongly disapprove and cannot go along with it.*
8. *I will be so seriously upset I can't predict my reaction.*
9. *No possible way! If you do, I quit.*
10. *Over my dead body!*

It's simple but effective in getting couples talking and being a bit more objective—not to mention bending, not breaking. You can download the card for free at LesAndLeslie.com.

———————

"The marital relationship is the axis around which all other family relationships are formed," said Virginia Satir, widely regarded as the mother of family therapy. "The mates are the architects of the family." So true. And as you champion the architects in your counseling office, keep in mind that they are not only inexorably connected to the families they came from but also to the family they are building, from generation to generation.

CONCLUSION

IT'S EASIER THAN EVER

If I have seen further, it is by standing
on the shoulders of giants.
—*Isaac Newton*

Right at the top, in our introduction, we admitted that this book was in no way exhaustive. Tens of thousands of marriage researchers and hundreds of thousands of other studies deserve to be included. This book has only touched the surface of the science of lasting love. More studies emerge every week. New knowledge will be acquired.

But the science we've presented in these pages is more than enough to demonstrate that we—marriage champions—have what it takes to help couples enjoy lasting love. In fact, it's never been easier. We stand on a massive mountain of evidence. We're privy to vistas that allow us to see marriage like never before. Previous generations have only dreamed of discovering what we now know. And what we know works. We have time-tested and ever-evolving tools that make our efforts more and more effective. Whether you are a clinical psychologist with a PhD, a volunteer marriage mentor, or a member of the clergy, you can work with confidence, empowering couples.

Einstein said, "If we knew what it was we were doing, it would not be called research, would it?" Well, at this point we've done enough research on marriage to have a pretty good idea of what we are doing. Research will continue, but we have enough evidence to know our efforts with couples can produce meaningful and powerful results.

Truly, it's never been easier to help couples enjoy lasting love. And with this in mind, we leave you with three hopes.

We Hope You Know What Matters Most

In 1937, a researcher at Harvard University began a study on what factors contribute to well-being and happiness. The research team selected 268 Harvard students who seemed healthy and well-adjusted to be part of a longitudinal study, meaning that the researchers would study the lives of these people not just at one point in time, but rather over a period of time. In this case, the period of time has been extraordinary— more than seventy years.

It's one of the most in-depth and important psychological studies of our time. With decades of perspective, the study gives a comprehensive viewpoint on what affects the level of health and happiness over a lifetime. It has tracked an array of factors, including physical exercise, cholesterol levels, marital status, the use of alcohol, smoking, education, and weight, but also more subjective psychological factors such as how a person copes with the challenges of life.

Over the last forty-two years, the director of this study has been psychiatrist George Vaillant. Someone asked Dr. Vaillant what he had learned about human health and happiness from his years of poring over the data on these people. You would expect a complex answer from a Harvard social scientist, but his secret to happiness was breathtakingly simple: "The only thing that really matters in life are your relationships."[1]

That's it: relationships. The most in-depth study ever conducted on the well-being of humans sums up what matters most with that single word. It's not surprising, really, is it? As researchers have pursued the age-old mystery of what makes people most fulfilled, what appears consistently at the top of the charts is not success, wealth, achievement, good looks, or any of those enviable assets. It's always *relationships*. Close ones. In fact, marriage is the centerpiece of close relationships. For it's in the context of marriage that our deepest fulfillments are met.

Never forget that your work as a marriage champion matters. You are touching lives where it matters most. You're not dabbling with frivolity; you're deep in the core of what brings abiding joy and meaning. You're adding life-changing significance and value to people's lives. You're doing noble work. You're walking on sacred ground. Love. It's the ultimate good. "The most excellent way."

We Hope You're Awestruck

Richard P. Feynman, a theoretical physicist known for his work in quantum mechanics, wrote a book called *The Pleasure of Finding Things Out*.[2] In it, he describes an exchange with a friend who's an artist. "He'll hold up a flower and say, 'look how beautiful it is,' and I'll agree," writes Feynman. "Then he says, 'I as an artist can see how beautiful this is but you as a scientist take this all apart and it becomes a dull thing,' and I think that he's kind of nutty."

Feynman goes on to say that the beauty that the artist sees is available to everyone. "Although I may not be quite as refined aesthetically as he is, I can appreciate the beauty of a flower." But Feynman also says that he can see much more in the flower than the artist sees. Feynman says he can imagine the cells in the flower, its internal complexity, which also have a beauty. Feynman, the scientist, says he sees beauty on a different dimension, the beauty of the flower's inner structure and workings. "The fact that the colors in the flower evolved in order to attract insects to pollinate it is interesting," he muses. "All kinds of interesting questions arise, and science only adds to the excitement, the mystery and the awe of a flower."

Marriage, like the flower, is forever mysterious and wonderful. Putting it under the proverbial microscope of science only makes it more so. Discovering its intricacies and learning more about its inner workings captivates us all the more. And we hope it does the same for you. The science of lasting love adds to the beauty of this God-given gift called marriage. Think of it. We join our life to the life of another human soul and share a connection that only the two of us can fully understand or ever appreciate. Amazing.

We Hope You'll Replicate Yourself

Ever heard of the *shampoo algorithm*? You undoubtedly have, even if you don't know the term. It's simple: wash, rinse, repeat. This little idiom is found on nearly every bottle of shampoo in the world. But it's used these days less as an instruction and more as a humorous way of pointing out its absurdity. Taken literally, it would result in an endless loop of repeating the same steps until the shampoo runs out.

Well, we're proposing a *marriage algorithm*, and we don't think it's that absurd. Remember how we noted that couples wait an average of six years to get help from someone like you? And as you know, the vast majority of engaged couples don't get premarital education. The need is so vast, and there are so few to help. So, first, we hope that you're doing what you can to make your services known—so you can reach more couples. Couples need you. And second, we hope you'll recruit more marriage champions. The world needs more of you.

———

We have to say it one more time: *Thank you*. It wouldn't be right to close this book without underscoring our gratitude for you again. As we noted in the introduction, we wish we knew you personally, by name, and could put you on the dedication page. You are the reason we wrote this book. Our hearts are filled with gratitude for your passion, your skills, and your efforts to help couples enjoy lasting love. We can't say it enough: Thank you. We are here for you, pulling for you, every step of the way, as you help the couples in your care.

To-do List

❤

☑ Read <u>Helping Couples</u>

☐ Visit Loveology.org

Wondering what's next? Visit **loveology.org**

loveology»

Because you're there for them ...

The help you need,
as a marriage champion,
from the experts you trust.

loveology»

... we're here for you.

- Multiply your effectiveness
- Boost your confidence
- Increase your retention
- Learn new techniques

Always free

loveology.org

ABOUT THE AUTHORS

Les Parrott, PhD, & Leslie Parrott, EdD, are founders of the SYMBIS Assessment. A psychologist and marriage and family therapist, respectfully, and #1 *New York Times* bestselling authors, Les and Leslie have more than six million copies of their books in print, in more than two dozen languages. Titles include *Love Talk*, *The Good Fight*, *Trading Places*, and the Gold Medallion Book Award–winning *Saving Your Marriage Before It Starts*. The governor of Oklahoma appointed the Parrotts as the first ever statewide marriage ambassadors. Drs. Parrott have been featured in *USA Today* and the *New York Times* and have appeared on CNN, Fox News, *Good Morning America*, the *Today* show, *The View*, and *Oprah*.

David H. Olson, PhD, is founder of the PREPARE/ENRICH assessment. A family science pioneer and an international marriage expert, Olson is professor emeritus at the University of Minnesota, where he taught for thirty years. Known for bridging research, theory, and practice, his Circumplex Model of Marital and Family Systems is one of the most popular and scientifically tested models for understanding and treating couples and families. David has written over one hundred journal articles and more than twenty books. His titles include *Marriages and Families, Empowering Couples,* and *The Couple Checkup.* Dr. Olson has appeared on a variety of programs including the *Today* show, *CBS This Morning, Good Morning America,* and *Oprah.*

NOTES

Introduction

1. Eli J. Finkel, Paul W. Eastwick, and Harry T. Reis (2015), "Best Research Practices in Psychology: Illustrating Epistemological and Pragmatic Considerations with the Case of Relationship Science," *Journal of Personality and Social Psychology*, 108, no. 2 (February 2015): 275–97.

Chapter 1: Love Is Not Enough

1. This is not a new phenomenon. A poll taken in 1966 reported that 76 percent of the married couples questioned named "love" as the major reason for marrying. Ten years later, in 1976, when a psychologist asked seventy-five thousand wives to evaluate the reasons for their decision to wed, she reported: "Love, love, love was far and away the front-runner." Paul Chance, "The Trouble with Love," *Psychology Today* (February 1988): 44–47.

2. Stephanie Coontz, "The World Historical Transformation of Marriage," *Journal of Marriage and Family* 66, no. 4, (November 2004): 974–79.

3. Daniel B. Wile, "Collaborative Couple Therapy," in *Clinical Handbook of Couple Therapy*, 3rd ed., ed. Alan S. Gurman and Neil S. Jacobson (New York: Guilford, 2002), 281–307.

4. Victor Karandashev, "A Cultural Perspective on Romantic

Love," *Online Readings in Psychology and Culture* 5, no. 4 (June 2015), https://doi.org/10.9707/2307-0919.1135.

5. Eli J. Finkel, *The All or Nothing Marriage* (New York: Dutton, 2017).

6. Andreas Bartels, and Semir Zeki, "The Neural Basis of Romantic Love," *NeuroReport: For Rapid Communication of Neuroscience Research* 11, no. 17 (November 27, 2000): 3829–34. Andreas Bartels and Semir Zeki, "The Neural Correlates of Maternal and Romantic Love," *NeuroImage* 21, no. 3 (March 2004): 1155–1166.

7. George F. Koob, and Nora D. Volkow, "Neurocircuitry of Addiction," *Neuropsychopharmacology* 35 (August 2009): 217–38. And Stephanie Ortigue et al., "Neuroimaging of Love: fMRI Meta-Analysis Evidence toward New Perspectives in Sexual Medicine," *Journal of Sexual Medicine* 7, no. 11 (November 2010): 3541–52.

8. Dr. Helen Fisher, an anthropologist and relationship researcher, conducted a series of illuminating studies on the brain chemistry of love. Specifically, she found that the same brain chemicals (that is, massive amounts of dopamine and norepinephrine) are in play, and many of the same brain pathways and structures are active when we are falling in love and enjoying a cocaine-high. Helen Fisher, "Lust, Attraction, Attachment: Biology and Evolution of the Three Primary Emotion Systems for Mating, Reproduction, and Parenting," *Journal of Sex Education and Therapy* 25, no. 1 (2000): 96–104.

9. Inna Schneiderman et al., "Oxytocin during the Initial Stages of Romantic Attachment: Relations to Couples' Interactive Reciprocity," *Psychoneuroendocrinology* 37, no. 8 (August 2012): 1277–85.

10. Bianca P. Acevedo and Arthur Aron (2009), "Does a Long-Term Relationship Kill Romantic Love?" *Review of General Psychology* 13, no. 1 (2009): 59–65, https://www.apa.org/pubs/journals/releases/gpr13159.pdf.

11. "How Important Is Romance to You in a Relationship?" Statista Research Department, December 12, 2009, https://www.statista.com/statistics/243663/importance-of-romance-in-a-relationship-in-the-united-states/.

12. Terry Gaspard, "Timing Is Everything When It Comes to Marriage Counseling," *Gottman Relationship Blog*, July 23, 2015, https://www.gottman.com/blog/timing-is-everything-when-it-comes-to-marriage-counseling/.

13. Paul R. Amato et al., *Alone Together: How Marriage in America Is Changing* (Cambridge, MA: Harvard University Press, 2007).

14. Blaine J. Fowers and David H. Olson (1989), "ENRICH Marital Inventory: A Discriminant Validity and Cross-Validation Assessment," *Journal of Marital and Family Therapy* 15, no. 1 (January 1989): 65–79, https://doi.org/10.1111/j.1752-0606.1989.tb00777.x.

15. David H. Olson et al., *Comparison of Five Premarital Approaches Using PREPARE. Final Report*, (Minneapolis: PREPARE-ENRICH, 1979).

16. Jennifer M. Bonds-Raacke et al., "Engaging Distortions: Are We Idealizing Marriage?" *The Journal of Psychology Interdisciplinary and Applied* 135, no. 2 (2001): 179–84.

17. In this case, results demonstrated that individuals engaged to be married had significantly higher idealistic distortion scores (M = 86.89) than did either married individuals (M = 56.67) or those in extended dating relationships. Also see Acevedo and Aron, "Does a Long-Term Relationship Kill Romantic Love?" 59–65.

18. Donald H. Baucom et al., "Cognitive-Behavioral Couple Therapy" in *Handbook of Cognitive-Behavioral Therapies*, 3rd ed., ed. Keith S. Dobson (New York: Guilford, 2009), 411–44

19. Paul W. Eastwick et al., "The Predictive Validity of Ideal Partner Preferences: A Review and Meta-Analysis," *Psychological Bulletin* 140, no. 3 (May 2014): 623–65.

20. Les Parrott and Leslie Parrott, *Saving Your Marriage Before It Starts*, rev. ed. (Grand Rapids. MI: Zondervan, 2015).

Chapter 2: The 31 Percent Factor

1. "Ernest R. and Gladys Groves Papers," Institute for Regional Studies & University Archives, North Dakota State University Libraries (2009), https://library.ndsu.edu/ir/bitstream /handle/10365/203/Mss0169.pdf?sequence=7.

2. By the eighth century, marriage was widely accepted in the Catholic church as a sacrament, or a ceremony to bestow God's grace. At the Council of Trent in 1563, the sacramental nature of marriage was written into canon law.

3. Robert F. Stahmann and Connie J. Salts, "Educating for Marriage and Intimate Relationships," in *Handbook of Family Life Education*, ed. Margaret E. Arcus, Jay D. Schvaneveldt, and J. Joel Moss, vol. 2 (Newbury Park, CA: Sage Publications, 1993).

4. Robert Latou Dickinson, "Premarital Examination as Routine Preventive Gynecology," *American Journal of Obstetrics and Gynecology* 16, no. 5 (November 1, 1928): 631–41, https:// www.ajog.org/article/S0002-9378(28)90773-5/abstract.

5. E. Mudd, C. Freeman, and E. Rose (1941), "Premarital Counseling in the Philadelphia Marriage Council," *Mental Hygiene* 25 (1941), 98–119.

6. Kristin Celello, *Making Marriage Work: A History of Marriage and Divorce in the Twentieth-Century United States* (Chapel Hill, NC: The University of North Carolina Press, 2009).

7. Stahmann and Salts, "Educating for Marriage and Intimate Relationships."

8. Orit Avishai, Melanie Heath, and Jennifer Randles, "Marriage Promotion Policy," in *The Wiley Blackwell Encyclopedia of Family Studies*, ed. Constance L. Shehan, vol. 3 (Hoboken, NJ: Wiley-Blackwell, 2016), 1374–78.

9. Coalition for Marriage, Family, and Couples Education et al.,

The Marriage Movement: A Statement of Principles (New York: Institute for American Values, 2000), http://americanvalues .org/catalog/pdfs/marriagemovement.pdf.

10. John M. Gottman and Clifford I. Notarius, "Marital Research in the 20th Century and a Research Agenda for the 21st Century," *Family Process* 41, no. 2 (Summer 2002): 159–97.

11. Deborah Schupack, "'Starter Marriages': So Early, So Brief," *New York Times*, July 7, 1994, https://www.nytimes .com/1994/07/07/garden/starter-marriages-so-early-so -brief.html.

12. Martin King Whyte, *Myth of the Social Volcano* (Stanford, CA: Stanford University Press, 2010); also Martin King Whyte, "The State of Marriage in America," in *Marriage in America: A Communitarian Perspective.* (Lanham, MD: Rowman and Littlefield, 2000).

13. Harbour Fraser Hodder, "The Future of Marriage," Harvard Magazine, November/December 2004, https://www .harvardmagazine.com/2004/11/the-future-of-marriage.html.

14. Theodore F. Robles, "Marital Quality and Health: Implications for Marriage in the 21st Century," *Current Directions in Psychological Science* 23, no. 6 (December 2014): 427–432, https://doi.org/10.1177/0963721414549043.

15. Linda J. Waite and Maggie Gallagher, *The Case for Marriage: Why Married People Are Happier, Healthier, and Better Off Financially* (New York: Doubleday, 2001).

16. Stephen F. Duncan, "How to Increase Participation in Marriage and Relationship Education," *Institute for Family Studies Blog*, March 15, 2018, from https://ifstudies.org/blog /how-to-increase-participation-in-marriage-and-relationship -education-programs.

17. Scott M. Stanley et al., "Premarital Education, Marital Quality, and Marital Stability: Findings from a Large, Random, Household Survey," *Journal of Family Psychology* 20, no. 1 (March 2006): 117–126.

18. Hodder, "The Future of Marriage."

19. Brian J. Willoughby and Spencer L. James, *The Marriage Paradox: Why Emerging Adults Love Marriage Yet Push It Aside* (New York, NY: Oxford University Press, 2017).

20. Les Parrott and Leslie Parrott, "Preparing Couples for Marriage: The SYMBIS Model" in *Evidence Based Practices for Christian Counseling and Psychotherapy*, ed. Everett L.Worthington Jr. et al., (Downers Grove, IL: InterVarsity, 2013); and Les Parrott and Leslie Parrot, "Preparing Couples for Marriage: The SYMBIS Model," in *Case Studies in Couples Therapy: Theory-Based Approaches*, ed. David K. Carson and Montserrat Casado-Kehoe (New York: Routledge, 2011), 13–27.

21. Scott M. Stanley et al., "Best Practices in Relationship Education Focused on Intimate Relationships," *Family Relations* 69, no. 3 (July 2020): 497–219, https://doi.org/10.1111/fare.12419.

22. Patrick Fagan, Robert Patterson, and Robert Rector, "Marriage and Welfare Reform: The Overwhelming Evidence that Marriage Education Works," The Heritage Foundation, October 25, 2002, https://www.heritage.org/welfare/report/marriage-and-welfare-reform-the-overwhelming-evidence-marriage-education-works.

23. Stanley et al., "Premarital Education, Marital Quality, and Marital Stability."

24. Paul Giblin, Douglas H. Sprenkle, and Robert Sheehan,, "Enrichment Outcome Research: A Meta-Analysis of Premarital, Marital, and Family Interventions," *Journal of Marital and Family Therapy* 11, no. 13 (1985): 257–271.

25. Jason S. Carroll and William J. Doherty, "Evaluating the Effectiveness of Premarital Prevention Programs: A Meta-Analytic Review of Outcome Research," *Family Relations* 52, no. 2 (2003): 105–18, https://doi.org/10.1111/j.1741-3729.2003.00105.x.

26. Luke Knutson and David H. Olson, "Effectiveness of the PREPARE Program with Premarital Couples in Community Settings," *Marriage & Family: A Christian Journal* 6, no. 4 (2003): 529–46, https://www.prepare-enrich.com/pe/pdf/research/aacc_study_2003.pdf.

27. Carroll and Doherty, "Evaluating the Effectiveness of Premarital Prevention Programs."

28. Alan J. Hawkins and Sage E. Erickson (2015), "Is Couple and Relationship Education Effective for Lower Income Participants? A Meta-Analytic Study," *Journal of Family Psychology*, 29, no. 1 (February 2015): 59–68. And Elizabeth B. Fawcett et al., "Do Premarital Education Programs Really Work? A Meta-Analytic Study," *Family Relations: An Interdisciplinary Journal of Applied Family Studies* 59, no. 3 (July 2010): 232–39, https://doi.org/10.1111/j.1741-3729.2010.00598.x.

29. Casey E. Copen, Kimberly Daniels, and William D. Mosher, "First Premarital Cohabitation in the United States: 2006–2010 National Survey of Family Growth," *National Health Statistics Reports* 64 (April 4, 2013): 1–15.

30. Galena K. Rhoades, Scott M. Stanley, and Howard J. Markman (2009), "Couples' Reasons for Cohabitation Associations with Individual Well-Being and Relationship Quality," *Journal of Family Issues* 30, no. 2 (February 1, 2009): 233–58.

31. http://nationalmarriageproject.org/reports.

32. Galena H. Kline et al., "Timing Is Everything: Pre-Engagement Cohabitation and Increased Risk for Poor Marital Outcomes," *Journal of Family Psychology* 18, no. 2 (June 2004): 311–18.

33. Scott M. Stanley, Galena K. Rhoades, and Howard J. Markman (2006), "Sliding Versus Deciding: Inertia and the Premarital Cohabitation Effect," *Family Relationship* 55, no. 4 (October 2006): 499–509.

34. Michael J. Rosenfeld and Katharina Roesler, "Cohabitation Experience and Cohabitation's Association with Marital Dissolution," *Journal of Marriage and Family* 81, no. 1 (February 2019): 42–58.

35. Peter J. Larson and David H. Olson, "Cohabitation and Relationship Quality in Dating and Engaged Couples," PREPARE/ENRICH, https://www.prepare-enrich.com/pe /pdf/research/cohab_relat_qual.pdf.

36. Claire M. Kamp Dush, Catherine L. Cohan, and Paul R. Amato, "The Relationships between Cohabitation and Marital Quality and Stability: Change across Cohorts?" *Journal of Marriage and Family* 65, no. 3 (August 2003): 539–549; and Scott M. Stanley et al., "The Timing of Cohabitation and Engagement: Impact on First and Second Marriages," *Journal of Marriage and Family* 72, no. 4 (August 2010): 906–18.

37. Annie C. Hsueh, Kristen Rahbar Morrison, and Brian D. Doss (2009), "Qualitative Reports of Problems in Cohabiting Relationships: Comparisons to Married and Dating Relationships," *Journal of Family Psychology* 23, no. 2 (April 2009): 236–46.

38. Stephanie Coontz, *The Way We Never Were: American Families and the Nostalgia Trap.*, rev. ed. (New York: Basic Books, 2016).

39. There is one divorce approximately every thirty-six seconds. That's nearly 2,400 divorces per day, 16,800 divorces per week, and 876,000 divorces a year. Cumulatively, one in every four families will face divorce; of this half, close to 50 percent will also see the breakup of a parent's second marriage. See "Marriage and Divorce," Centers for Disease Control and Prevention, https://www.cdc.gov/nchs/fastats/marriage -divorce.htm.

Chapter 3: Awareness Is Curative

1. The grant came from the Blandin Foundation, which was founded in 1941 by Charles K. Blandin and continues to

generously support the local community and beyond to this day.

2. David H. Olson et al., *Comparison of Five Premarital Approaches Using PREPARE. Final Report.* (Minneapolis: PREPARE-ENRICH, 1979).

3. Learn more at SYMBIS.com as well as: Les Parrott and Leslie Parrott, "Preparing Couples for Marriage: The SYMBIS Model," in *Evidence-Based Practices for Christian Counseling and Psychotherapy*, ed. Everett L. Worthington Jr. et al., (Downers Grove, IL: InterVarsity Press, 2013); and L. Parrott and L. Parrott, "Preparing Couples for Marriage: The SYMBIS Model," in *Case Studies in Couples Therapy: Theory-Based Approaches*, ed. David K. Carson and Montserrat Casado-Kehoe (New York, NY: Routledge, 2011), 13–27; L. Parrott and L. Parrott (2006), "Advances in the SYMBIS Approach to Marriage Education," *Marriage and Family: A Christian Journal* (2006); L. Parrott and L. Parrott (2003), "The SYMBIS Approach to Marriage Education," *Journal of Psychology and Theology*, 31, no. 3 (September 2003): 208–212; and J. S. Ripley et al., "An Initial Evaluation of the Parrotts' Saving Your Marriage Before It Starts (SYMBIS) Seminar: Who Benefits?" *Marriage and Family: A Christian Journal*, 3 (2000): 83–96.

4. Stephen F. Duncan, Geniel R. Childs, and Jeffry H. Larson (2010), "Perceived Helpfulness of Four Different Types of Marriage Preparation Interventions," *Family Relations* 59, no. 5 (December 2010): 623–36.

5. Everett L. Worthington Jr. et al., "Can Couple Assessment and Feedback Improve Relationships? Assessment as a Brief Relationship Enrichment Procedure," *Journal of Counseling Psychology* 42, no. 4 (1995):466–75; Jeffry H. Larson et al., "The Relationship Evaluation (RELATE) with Therapist-Assisted Interpretation: Short-Term Effects on Premarital Relationships," *Journal of Marital and Family Therapy* 33, no. 3

(July 2007): 364–74; and Luke Knutson and David H. Olson, "Effectiveness of PREPARE Program with Premarital Couples in Community Settings," *Marriage & Family: A Christian Journal* 6, no. 4 (2003): 529–46, https://www .prepare-enrich.com/pe/pdf/research/aacc_study_2003.pdf.

6. David H. Olson, "Value of PREPARE Program in Preventing Divorce" (Minneapolis, MN: Life Innovations, 2020).

7. Tasha Eurich, "What Self-Awareness Really Is (and How to Cultivate It)," *Harvard Business Review*, January 4, 2018, https://hbr.org/2018/01/what-self-awareness-really-is -and-how-to-cultivate-it.

8. Philippe Rochat (2003), "Five Levels of Self-Awareness as They Unfold Early in Life," *Consciousness and Cognition* 12, no. 4 (December 2003): 717–31; and Shelley Duval and Robert A. Wicklund, *A Theory of Objective Self-Awareness*, (Ann Arbor, MI: Academic Press, 1972).

9. Les Parrott and Leslie Parrott, *Trading Places: The Secret to the Marriage You Want* (Grand Rapids, MI: Zondervan, 2008).

10. See Daniel Golman's groundbreaking book, *Social Intelligence* (New York: Bantam, 2007), where he unpacks in detail the new science of human relationships.

11. See J. Stuart Ablon and Carl D. Marci, "Psychotherapy Process: The Missing Link: Comment on Western, Novotny, and Thompson-Brenner (2004)," *Psychological Bulletin* 130, no. 4 (2004): 664–68; and Carl D. Marci, Erin K. Moran, Scott P. Orr, "Physiologic Evidence for the Interpersonal Role of Laughter During Psychotherapy," *Journal of Nervous and Mental Disease* 192, no. 10 (2004): 689–95.

12. J. S. Morris et al., "Differential Extrageniculostriate and Amygdala Responses to Presentation of Emotional Faces in a Cortically Blind Field," *Brain* 124, no. 6 (June 2001): 1241–52, https://doi.org/10.1093/brain/124.6.1241; Ablon and Marci, "Psychotherapy Process: The Missing Link"; Marci, "Physiologic Evidence for the Interpersonal Role of Laughter";

and Janice Kiecolt-Glaser et al. "Marital Stress: Immunologic, Neuroendocrine, and Autonomic Correlates," *Annals of the New York Academy of Sciences* 840, no. 1 (May 1998): 656–63.

13. Blaine J. Fowers and David H. Olson, "Predicting Marital Success with PREPARE: A Predictive Validity Study," *Journal of Marital and Family Therapy* 12, no. 4 (October 1986): 403–13.

14. While the name of the instrument is now PREPARE/ENRICH, it was the PREPARE version of the assessment that was used in this study. PREPARE refers to the original premarital-specific iteration of the current PREPARE/ENRICH customized assessment.

15. Knutson and Olson, "Effectiveness of PREPARE Program with Premarital Couples in Community Settings."

Chapter 4: Every Marriage Is Unique

1. Of course, genes do not account for all of personality—just the seeds of it. Environment also plays a significant role. Scientists' unwieldy name for this exchange is "evocative gene-environment correlations," so called because people's genetic makeup is thought to bring forth particular reactions from others, which in turn influence their personalities.

2. Robert Plomin et al., *Behavioral Genetics*, 5th ed. (New York, NY: Worth Publishers, 2008).

3. Robert Plomin and John R. Nesselroade, "Behavioral Genetics and Personality Change," *Journal of Personality* 58, no. 1 (March 1990): 191–220.

4. Which is why DNA left at a crime scene can be strongly linked to one individual.

5. Howard S. Friedman and Miriam W. Schustack, *Personality: Classic Theories and Modern Research*, 6th ed. (New York: Pearson, 2015); Richard A. Grucza and Lewis R. Goldberg, "The Comparative Validity of 11 Modern Personality

Inventories: Predictions of Behavioral Acts, Informant Reports, and Clinical Indicators," *Journal of Personality Assessment* 89, no. 2 (October 2007): 167–87; Lewis R. Goldberg, "The Structure of Phenotypic Personality Traits," *American Psychologist* 48, no. 1 (1993): 21–36; and Gerard Saucier and Lewis R. Goldberg, "The Language of Personality: Lexical Perspectives on the Five-Factor Model," in *The Five-Factor Model of Personality: Theoretical Perspectives*, ed. Jerry S. Wiggins (New York: Guilford, 1996), 21–49.

6. William M. Marston, *Emotions of Normal People* (1928; repr., Minneapolis: Persona, 1979); Peter F. Merenda and Walter V. Clarke, "Self Description and Personality Measurement," *Journal of Clinical Psychology* 21, no. 1 (January 1965): 52–56; and Janet M. (2006), "Making the Connection: Improving Virtual Team Performance through Behavioral Assessment Profiling and Behavioral Cues," *Developments in Business Simulation and Experiential Learning* 33 (2006): 358–59.

7. See Marston, *Emotions of Normal People*.

8. David H. Olson and Amy K. Olson, *Empowering Couples* (Minneapolis: Life Innovations, 2000).

9. Daniel Goleman, "Long-Married Couples Do Look Alike, Study Finds," *New York Times*, August 11, 1987, https://www.nytimes.com/1987/08/11/science/long-married-couples-do-look-alike-study-finds.html.

Chapter 5: Intimacy Requires Two Keys

1. Robert J. Sternberg, "Triangulating Love," in *The Altruism Reader: Selections from Writings on Love, Religion, and Science*, ed. Thomas Jay Oord (West Conshohocken, PA: Templeton, 2007), 331–47; and Robert J. Sternberg, "A Triangular Theory of Love," in *Close Relationships: Key Readings*, ed. Harry T. Reis and Caryl E. Rusbult (New York: Psychology, 2004), 213–38.

2. Alexandra E. Mitchell et al., "Predictors of Intimacy

in Couples' Discussions of Relationship Injuries: An Observational Study," *Journal of Family Psychology* 22, no. 1 (2008): 21–29, https://doi.org/10.1037/0893-3200.22.1.21.

3. Christopher R. Agnew et al., "Cognitive Interdependence: Commitment and the Mental Representation of Close Relationships," *Journal of Personality and Social Psychology* 74, no. 4 (1998): 939–54.

4. Jean-Philippe Laurenceau et al., "Intimacy as an Interpersonal Process: Current Status and Future Directions," in *Handbook of Closeness and Intimacy*, ed. Debra J. Mashek and Arthur Aron (Mahwah, NJ: Erlbaum, 2004), 61–78.

5. Daniel J. Hruschka, *Friendship: Development, Ecology, and Evolution of a Relationship*, vol. 5 (Berkeley, CA: University of California Press, 2010).

6. Karen J. Prager and Linda J. Roberts, "Deep Intimate Connection: Self and Intimacy in Couple Relationships," in *Handbook of Closeness and Intimacy*, ed. Debra J. Mashek and Arthur Aron (Mahwah, NJ: Erlbaum, 2004), 43–60.

7. When divorced couples are asked about the cause, 5 percent say it was due to physical abuse; 16 percent due to drug or alcohol abuse; and 17 percent due to adultery. The overwhelming cause of divorce reported by those who went through it was "incompatibility"—failure to simply get along together. As one report of these findings puts it, "Stated differently, three-fifths of marriages failed due to poor communication or conflict resolution skills" (Michael McManus and Harriet McManus, "How to Create an America That Saves Marriages," *Journal of Psychology and Theology* 31, no. 3 [September 2003]: 203)—reason enough for any marriage counselor to want to thoroughly understand communication training for couples.

8. Kira S. Birditt et al., "The Development of Marital Tension: Implications for Divorce among Married Couples," *Developmental Psychology* 53, no. 10 (2017): 1995–2006.

9. Valerian J. Derlega et al., "Developing Close Relationships," in *Self-Disclosure, Sage Series on Close Relationships* (Newbury Park, CA: Sage, 1993), 8–43.

10. James V. Cordova, Christina B. Gee, and Lisa Z. Warren, "Emotional Skillfulness in Marriage: Intimacy as a Mediator of the Relationship between Emotional Skillfulness and Marital Satisfaction," *Journal of Social and Clinical Psychology* 24, no. 2 (2005): 218–35.

11. Susan M. Johnson, *Attachment Theory in Practice: Emotionally Focused Therapy (EFT) with Individuals, Couples, and Families.* (New York: Guilford Press, 2019).

12. Stephen W. Porges, "Emotion: An Evolutionary By-Product of the Neural Regulation of the Autonomic Nervous System," *Annals of the New York Academy of Sciences* 807, no. 1 (January 15, 1997): 62–77; Stephen W. Porges, "Love: An Emergent Property of the Mammalian Autonomic Nervous System," *Psychoneuroendocrinology* 23, no. 8 (November 1998): 837–61; and Stephen W. Porges (2001), "The Polyvagal Theory: Phylogenetic Substrates of a Social Nervous System," *International Journal of Psychophysiology* 42, no. 2 (October 2001): 123–46.

13. Donald H. Baucom et al., "Long-Term Prediction of Marital Quality following a Relationship Education Program: Being Positive in a Constructive Way," *Journal of Family Psychology* 20, no. 3 (2006): 448–55; and Elizabeth A. Schilling et al., "Altering the Course of Marriage: The Effect of PREP Communication Skills Acquisition on Couples' Risk of Becoming Maritally Distressed," *Journal of Family Psychology* 17, no. 1 (March 2003): 41–53.

14. See William M. Marston, *Emotions of Normal People* (1928; repr., Minneapolis: Persona, 1979); Walter V. Clarke, *Basic Theory, Administration, and Application of Activity Vector Analysis* (Barrington, RI: Walter V. Clarke Associates, 1967); Bill J. Bonnstetter, Judy Suiter, and Randy J. Widrick, *The*

Universal Language, DISC: A Reference Manual (Scottsdale: Target Training, 2001); Michael O'Connor, *The DISC Model, Trainer and Consultant Reference Encyclopedia* (New York: Life Associates, 1987); C. G. Jung, *Psychological Types*, The *Collected Works of C. G. Jung*, vol. 6 (Princeton: Princeton University Press, 1971); and John Trent and Rodney Cox, *Leading from Your Strengths* (Nashville: B&H, 2004).

15. Les Parrott and Leslie Parrott, *Love Talk: Speak Each Other's Language like You Never Have Before* (Grand Rapids, MI: Zondervan, 2019).

16. Paul Tournier, *To Understand Each Other* (Atlanta: John Knox Press, 1967), 29.

17. Theodor Reik, *Listening with the Third Ear: The Inner Experience of a Psychoanalyst* (New York: Farrar, Straus, 1949).

18. Les Parrott, *Counseling and Psychotherapy*, 2nd ed. (Bel Air: CA, Thomson/Brooks/Cole, 2003).

19. Virginia P. Richmond, James C. McCroskey, and K. David Roach, "Communication and Decision-Making Styles, Power Base Usage, and Satisfaction in Marital Dyads," *Communication Quarterly* 45, no. 4 (1997): 410–17.

20. Jeffry A. Simpson, M. Minda Oriña, and William Ickes, "When Accuracy Hurts, and When It Helps: A Test of the Empathic Accuracy Model in Marital Interactions," *Journal of Personality and Social Psychology* 85, no. 5 (2003): 881–93, https://doi.org/10.1037/0022-3514.85.5.881.

21. Les Parrott and Leslie Parrott, *The Good Fight: How Conflict Can Bring You Closer* (Nashville: Worthy, 2013).

22. "Fair Feud? Six Issues Couples Should Argue About," MSN .com, December 7, 2010; and "Men's Health on Which Arguments Can Ruin or Strengthen Relationships," MSN.com, August 20, 2007, http://today.msn.com/id/20323044.

23. Unhealthy conflict makes married couples more susceptible to illness and even prolongs the healing process of a wound. See Jan Kiecolt-Glaser et al., "Study Shows How Troubled

Marriage, Depression History Promote Obesity," Ohio State News, October 20, 2014, https://news.osu.edu/study-shows -how-troubled-marriage-depression-history-promote-obesity/.

24. Kim T. Buehlman and John Gottman, "The Oral History Coding System," in *What Predicts Divorce? The Measures*, ed. John Gottman (Hillsdale, NJ: Erlbaum, 1996).

25. Buehlman and Gottman, "The Oral History Coding System."

26. John Gottman and Joan DeClaire, *The Relationship Cure: A Five-Step Guide to Strengthening Your Marriage, Family, and Friendships* (New York: Crown, 2001).

27. John Gottman with Nan Silver, *Why Marriages Succeed or Fail: What You Can Learn from the Breakthrough Research to Make Your Marriage Last* (New York: Simon & Schuster, 1994).

28. Rachel A. Simmons, Peter C. Gordon, and Dianne L. Chambless, "Pronouns in Marital Interaction: What Do 'You' and 'I' Say about Marital Health?" *Psychological Science* 16, no. 12 (December 2005): 932–36.

29. Michael Fulwiler, "Managing Conflict: Solvable vs. Perpetual Problems," *Gottman Relationship Blog*, July 2, 2012, https:// www.gottman.com/blog/managing-conflict-solvable -vs-perpetual-problems/.

30. Paula Szuchman and Jenny Anderson, *Spousonomics: Using Economics to Master Love, Marriage, and Dirty Dishes* (New York: Random House, 2011).

31. Owen Ware, "Forgiveness and Respect for Persons," *American Philosophical Quarterly* 51, no. 3 (July 2014): 247–60.

32. This research led to the REACH Forgiveness method for psychoeducational groups. See Everett L. Worthington Jr., *Hope for Troubled Marriages: Overcoming Common Problems and Major Difficulties* (Downers Grove, IL: InterVarsity, 1993); Jennifer S. Ripley and Everett L Worthington Jr., *Couple Therapy: A New Hope-Focused Approach* (Downers Grove, IL: InterVarsity, 2014); Everett L. Worthington Jr.,

Jack W. Berry, and Les Parrott, "Unforgiveness, Forgiveness, Religion, and Health," in *Faith and Health: Psychological Perspectives*, ed. Thomas G. Plante and Allen C. Sherman (New York: Guilford, 2001), 107–38; Jack W. Berry et al., "Forgiveness, Vengeful Rumination, and Affective Traits," *Journal of Personality* 73, no. 1 (February 2005): 183–226; and Jack W. Berry et al., "Dispositional Forgiveness: Development and Construct Validity of the Transgression Narrative Test of Forgivingness (TNTF)," *Personality and Social Psychology Bulletin* 27, no. 10 (October 2001): 1277–90.

33. Sara D. Hodges and Kristi J. K. Klein, "Regulating the Costs of Empathy: The Price of Being Human," *Journal of Socio-Economics* 30, no. 5 (September–October 2001): 437–52; Frederique de Vignemont and Tania Singer, "The Empathic Brain: How, When and Why?" *Trends in Cognitive Sciences* 10, no. 10 (October 2006): 435–41; Nancy Eisenberg and Richard A. Fabes, "Empathy: Conceptualization, Measurement, and Relation to Prosocial Behavior," *Motivation and Emotion* 14 (June 1990): 131–49; and Adam D. Galinsky et al., "Why It Pays to Get Inside the Head of Your Opponent: The Differential Effects of Perspective Taking and Empathy in Negotiations," *Psychological Science* 19, no. 4 (April 2008): 378–84.

Chapter 6: Family Ties Pull Strings

1. Paul Pearsall, *The Power of the Family* (New York: Random House, 1991), 185.

2. Murray Bowen, "A Family Concept of Schizophrenia," in *The Etiology of Schizophrenia*, ed. Don D. Jackson (New York: Basic Books, 1960), 346–72.

3. The initial discovery of the three dimensions used with the Circumplex Model—cohesion, flexibility (initially called adaptability), and communication—was by David Olson. After listing more than two hundred concepts in the marital

and family therapy field, Dr. Olson found they clustered into the three dimensions of cohesion, flexibility, and communication. The three dimensions were discovered by clustering of concepts rather than empirical clustering. It is interesting that many family theorists have independently concluded that the dimensions were critical for understanding and treating marital and family systems. A second discovery, that cohesion and flexibility are curvilinear, occurred when the first author listed the concepts by various family professionals within a given dimension. Also of note is that although attempts were made conceptually to define communication in a curvilinear manner and to integrate communication as a third circumplex dimension, it became too confusing conceptually and empirically. The decision was made to keep communication as a linear dimension and consider it a facilitating dimension in moving couples and families on the two other dimensions.

4. Laura Waldvogel and Molly Schlieff, *Updated Circumplex Model studies, 2000–2018*. Unpublished manuscript. (Roseville, MN: PREPARE/ENRICH, 2018).

5. The most recent version (FACES IV) was designed to measure cohesion and flexibility in a curvilinear manner, tapping both high and low extremes of these two dimensions, as well as the moderate regions that had been tapped by previous versions. FACES IV measures both balanced and unbalanced aspects of family functioning and provides a comprehensive assessment of family cohesion and flexibility dimensions using six scales. The two balanced scales are Balanced Cohesion and Balanced Flexibility. The four new unbalanced scales are Enmeshed and Disengaged in relation to cohesion and Chaotic and Rigid in terms of flexibility. The original studies have reported that FACES IV is highly reliable in the six scales. David H. Olson, Douglas H. Sprenkle, and Candyce S. Russell, "Circumplex Model of Marital and Family Systems: I. Cohesion and

Adaptability Dimensions, Family Types, and Clinical Applications," *Family Process* 18, no. 1 (April 1979): 3–28. See David H. Olson, "Circumplex Model of Marital and Family Systems," *Journal of Family Therapy* 22, no. 2 (May 2000): 144–67; David H. Olson, *FACES IV Manual* (Minneapolis: Life Innovations, 2010); and David H. Olson, "FACES IV and the Circumplex Model: Validity Study," *Journal of Marital and Family Therapy* 3, no. 1 (2011): 64–80.

6. FACES was added to PREPARE/ENRICH in 1985.

7. Olson, "Circumplex Model of Marital and Family Systems."

8. David H. Olson, Laura Waldvogel, and Molly Schlieff, "Circumplex Model of Marital and Family Systems: An Update," *Journal of Family Theory & Review* 11, no. 2 (June 2019):199–211.

9. David H. Olson and Amy K. Olson, "PREPARE/ENRICH Program: Version 2000," in *Preventive Approaches in Couples Therapy*, ed. Rony Berger and Mo Therese Hannah (Philadelphia: Brunner/Mazel, 2013), 196–216.

10. Paul J. Zak, Angela A. Stanton, and Sheila Ahmadi, "Oxytocin Increases Generosity in Humans," PLoS One 2, no. 11 (November 2007): e1128, https://doi.org/10.1371 /journal.pone.0001128; and Jorge A. Barraza and Paul J. Zak, "Empathy toward Strangers Triggers Oxytocin Release and Subsequent Generosity," *Annals of the New York Academy of Sciences* 1167, no. 1 (June 2009): 182–89.

11. A. J. Tomarken et al., "Individual Differences in Anterior Brain Asymmetry and Fundamental Dimensions of Emotion," *Journal of Personality and Social Psychology* 62, no. 4 (1992): 676–87; and Heather L. Urry et al., "Making a Life Worth Living: Neural Correlates of Well-Being," *Psychological Science* 15, no. 6 (June 2004): 367–72. See also Jack van Honk and Dennis J. L. G. Schutter, "From Affective Valence to Motivational Direction: The Frontal Asymmetry of Emotion Revised," *Psychological Science* 17, no. 11 (November 2006): 963–65.

12. Albert Bandura, *Social Foundations of Thought and Action: A Social Cognitive Theory* (Englewood Cliffs, NJ: Prentice-Hall, 1986).

13. Ronald M. Sabatelli and Suzanne Bartle-Haring, "Family-of -Origin Experiences and Adjustment in Married Couples," *Journal of Marriage and Family* 65, no. 1 (February 2003): 159–69; and W. Kim Halford, Matthew R. Sanders, and Brett C. Behrens, "Repeating the Errors of Our Parents? Family-of -Origin Spouse Violence and Observed Conflict Management in Engaged Couples," *Family Process* 39, no. 2 (June 2000): 219–35.

14. Harry Benson and Steve McKay, "'Date Nights' Strengthen Marriages," Marriage Foundation, September 2016, https:// marriagefoundation.org.uk/wp-content/uploads/2016/09/MF -paper-Date-Nights-Sep-2016-1.pdf.

15. W. Bradford Wilcox and Jeffrey Dew, "The Date Night Opportunity: What Does Couple Time Tell Us About the Potential of Date Nights?" National Marriage Project, http:// nationalmarriageproject.org/wp-content/uploads/2012/05 /NMP-DateNight.pdf.

16. Arthur Aron et al., "Couples' Shared Participation in Novel and Arousing Activities and Experienced Relationship Quality," *Journal of Personality and Social Psychology* 78, no. 2 (2000): 273–84.

17. Duane W. Crawford et al., "Compatibility, Leisure, and Satisfaction in Marital Relationships," *Journal of Marriage and Family* 64, no. 2 (May 2002): 433–49.

18. Rand D. Conger et al., "Linking Economic Hardship to Marital Quality and Instability," *Journal of Marriage and Family* 52, no. 3 (August 1990): 643–56.

19. Benson and McKay, "'Date Nights' Strengthen Marriages."

20. Les Parrott and Leslie Parrott, *Making Happy: The Art and Science of a Happy Marriage* (Nashville: Worthy, 2014).

21. Allen Parducci, "Value Judgments: Toward a Relational

Theory of Happiness," in *Attitudinal Judgment*, ed. J. Richard Eiser (New York: Springer-Verlag, 1984), 3–21.

22. Rachel E. Dinero et al., "Influence of Family of Origin and Adult Romantic Partners on Romantic Attachment Security," *Journal of Family Psychology* 22, no. 4 (August 2008): 622–32, https://doi.org/10.1037/a0012506.

23. Olson, Waldvogel, and Schlieff, "Circumplex Model of Marital and Family Systems: An Update."

24. Dominik Schoebi, Benjamin R. Karney, and Thomas N. Bradbury, "Stability and Change in the First 10 Years of Marriage: Does Commitment Confer Benefits beyond the Effects of Satisfaction?" *Journal of Personality and Social Psychology* 102, no. 4 (April 2012): 729–42; J. Davila, Benjamin R. Karney, and Thomas N. Bradbury, "Attachment Change Processes in the Early Years of Marriage," *Journal of Personality and Social Psychology* 76, no. 5 (May 1999): 783–802; and Benjamin R. Karney and Thomas N. Bradbury, "Neuroticism, Marital Interaction, and the Trajectory of Marital Satisfaction," *Journal of Personality and Social Psychology* 72, no. 5 (May 1997): 1075–92.

25. Ellie Lisitsa, "Manage Conflict: The Art of Compromise," *Gottman Relationship Blog*, January 10, 2013, https://www.gottman.com/blog/manage-conflict-the-art-of-compromise/.

Conclusion

1. Joshua Wolf Shenk, "What Makes Us Happy?" *The Atlantic*, June 2009, 36–53, https://www.theatlantic.com/magazine/archive/2009/06/what-makes-us-happy/307439/.

2. Richard P. Feynman, *The Pleasure of Finding Things Out* (New York: Perseus, 1999), 2.